From Strings To Wings

PlaneTree

From Strings to Wings

by

X. Tawasentha

Published 2003
ISBN 1-84294-125-9

Published by PlaneTree

Old Station Offices,
Llanidloes,
Powys SY18 6EB
United Kingdom

Manufactured in the United Kingdom

This story is a compelling account of how X. Tawasentha's intended career as a professional violinist came to an early, and unexpected, halt.

At times with great humour, and at other times heartbreaking sadness, the reader shares in all the drama of a soul awakening to a new life, brought about by the arrival of first a duck, and then a dog.

Beautifully written, it is essential reading for all who care about living things, from ants and cats, to fields and trees, and will inspire the reader to see the world from an altered perspective.

Thank You

- to Hilda, for the many hours of time she has given to me;

- to Patricia, for all her encouragement and help;

- to Charles, for his computer skills in making this book a reality;

- to Jim Warren, for generously giving permission for his painting to be used on the cover of this book.
- http://www.jimwarren.com
-

PROLOGUE

Life is so much like a book, invisibly written in chapters and pages, and each book telling the life of a soul.

Like racks of volumes on library shelves, the books are all the same, just collections of typed and numbered pages, each with a varying cover.

Some books are long, others short, and yet amongst this vast array, no two will be identical, no two will tell the same story.

And so it is with humans.

With typical curiosity, surely all of us would be tempted to turn first, to the last chapter in the book of our life, to know the end of the tale.

What a pity that this "bird's eye" view can only come with age!

How wise all of us would be with hindsight!

Reading back through the book of my life, it seems that many of those pages turned almost too quickly for there to have been enough time to live through them!

Yet never was there an awareness of this, never a realisation of time slipping away without any chance of a re-living.

And now, as my own time slips towards its end, and eternity is a frequent thought, the realisation is acute that of all the varied gifts possessed by humans, time is the most precious gift of all.

Many of the pages in the book of my life, tell of an anger and a sadness that seemed, at times, to be almost insupportable.

But there are other pages filled with interest and achievement, and pervaded with hope.

It is my hope now, that in some small way, when my own time finally comes, I will leave this world a better place for having been here; that I will leave nothing behind me except footprints, that nothing will have been taken except photographs, and that I will have wasted nothing except time.

"I am the captain of my ship,
I am the master of my fate."

CHAPTER 1

At the start of my adult life - that of an eager and committed music student - the immediate importance of time was appreciated only in relation to bus and train timetables. If the first bus was late, then the connecting train was missed, and half an hour would be lost.

From the train to the second bus should have been a leisurely walk across the city, but too often, it ended up as a crazy sprint, pavements thickening with anxious morning commuters, traffic congestion increasing by the minute.

The domino effect of even one late bus would prove horrendous!

Did some early morning bus driver, starting his journey only a few minutes late, ever realise the consequences of his poor timekeeping?

Did he ever think that, at the end of my own journey, encumbered with a handbag, a violin, a carrier bag containing indoor shoes, and an over-filled and very heavy brief case, his lateness had made me more than an hour late?

I think not!

The solution to the time problem lay in bringing forward the morning marathon.

What could be better than to start the day with the last of the night-service buses?

So into the carrier bag, along with the shoes and all the other miscellaneous items, went a breakfast sandwich.

A practice room was booked at College from 7.30a.m. every morning, and the new regime was operational.

Living at home as a student had great benefits and advantages, as well as certain disadvantages. Amongst these latter, it seemed that secondary school had merely been exchanged for "tertiary" school. Life was still governed by parents, studies and exams, only the uniform was missing!

The "bohemian" life of the typical music student was unknown to me, all the problems of "bed-sitter land" lay in unknown territory, and social inter-action remained, as it had been in school days, none existent.

How distant those school days seem to me now, and yet how vivid!

I had been an unhappy child, and grew into a most unattractive teenager, with teenage troubles in abundance.

Looking back across the years, one can understand how the foundations of those troubles had been laid much earlier, whilst still a child.

The difficulties began with my father's change of job, and the upheavals of moving house, moving school, and starting a fresh life in a new area.

At the age of nine, I entered the prep school that was attached to a grammar school, where my older sister was already a pupil.

Suddenly, I had lost not only the first house I had ever known, with its familiar streets and pavements, and the friends with whom I had played, but also my school and its teachers, and all the reassuring routines of childhood.

It was here, for the first time in my young life, that I felt the unfamiliar hurt of rejection and unpopularity.

What was happening?

Why was I never chosen for team games?

Why could I not learn fast enough to fill the gaps in my previous knowledge?

And at this time my sister, an outstandingly clever girl - something only to be realised much later - would come home with glowing end-of-term reports, regularly sweeping the board at the annual prize nights.

Into this desert of unhappiness there fell a life-line of hope.

How often has it occurred to me, through the intervening years, that a miracle so often lies not in the event which actually happens, but in the precise timing of that event.

One day, into my classroom, came an elderly lady - the memory of her face is still held in my mind's eye - offering lunchtime violin lessons. A handful of girls volunteered, but by the end of the term, I was the only one who had not given up.

For the first time in my life, I was doing something in which my sister could not compete. Following an accident as an infant, she had lost the tip of her left index finger, yet even with this handicap, she had managed to be more successful in piano lessons than I had been.

At last, I could succeed in something!

Here was a pursuit that was mine, and mine alone.

No doubt, the noises coming from the music room must have sounded akin to chaos on a battlefield, but that dear old lady encouraged me, and I was naïve enough, and innocent enough, to believe in her words of encouragement.

Years passed, and I progressed into the grammar school, where the most frequent remark to be heard from the teachers was: "You're not like your sister, are you!"

Teenage problems intensified, and lack of friends, and unpopularity amongst other girls, inevitably led to withdrawal from a world in which I felt I was a freak, unwanted by everyone, and where it seemed I was destined never to succeed.

But there was to be an escape!

I was to find some measure of satisfaction and peace in the school library at first, and later on, in the local library.

I read Silas Marner, and was carried away into a world peopled with George Elliot's vividly drawn characters. Other great authors followed - Dickens, H.G.Wells, Jane Austen, the Bronte's, Mrs Gaskell, and so many more.

And at this time, too, although some poetry was studied for exam purposes, much more was read by choice. I walked in the magic worlds of Keats and Shelley, of Wordsworth, Milton and Browning. My soul expanded, gazing on Tintern Abbey, or viewing London's mean, dark streets from Westminster Bridge. I shared in Keats's wistful sadness, in Longfellows heroic Hiawatha, and in Tennyson's tumbling Brook, and his doomed Lady of Shallot. Even Dante's Divine Comedy was on my list, although it was never finished!

And all the while, I struggled on with the violin, practising scales and arpeggios, and listening to the great classical composers. Here, another world opened before me. Those long-suffering cleaners and caretakers allowed me into school for at least an hour's early morning violin practice, and in the evening, being allowed the use of the record library, they cleaned classrooms and polished corridors to the strains of Scherezade, and the Moldeau, and all the other great classical pieces. In stillness and often near darkness, I listened to Beethoven's symphonies, sharing with him the torment of his increasing deafness, and I strolled through the courts of emperors and kings to the elegant strains of Mozart.

At this time, Grandfather died very suddenly, on my sixteenth birthday.

He had been the guiding light, the restraining influence, on Grandmother, who was considerably older than him. Already suffering from mild dementia, Gran came to live with us.

The upset of not only losing Grandad, her soul-mate of over fifty years, but losing her own home where she and Grandad had lived for so many, happy years, caused serious damage to Gran's already fragile, mental state. Poor, dear Gran.

I paid little attention to her, wishing that she would talk less, move faster, and not get in my way.

How I wish I could re-live those years!

The first two years she was with us, were the years of my 'A' level exams. I spent them buried in Shakespeare, Elizabethan poetry, Latin and Music, and all the while, developing skill on the violin.

We used to laugh at Gran, who was a great cigarette smoker, as she carefully rolled up strips of newspaper, making them into tapers to light her cigarettes, then placing the tapers at the edge of the fire. No matter how often Dad would try to explain to her that the fire was electric, often dismantling it to show her that the coals were not hot, but only looked hot because they were lit from behind by a rotating red light bulb, Gran just could not understand.

4

All her life, she had raked cinders and stoked real coal fires, and as far as she was concerned, tapers could be lit from red hot coal. The workings of a look-alike electric fire were to remain a mystery to her for the rest of her life.

And at last, the time came for me to leave school. Having been accepted onto a degree course by a College of Music, I was elated, although my parents did not approve. They saw no safe career ahead, and considered my determination to proceed with music as a fanciful whim, taken to extremes. To be fair, though, they had never objected to the cost of private violin lessons during those school years, never objected to the endless hours of noise, and other than disapproving, they had never actively stood in my way. The highlight of student years was being in the official college orchestra.

Adrenalin levels went off the scale!

The excitement of "long-all-black" - which meant a black velvet evening skirt, a fancy black lace blouse, and black patent leather 'winkle-picker' shoes - was just the beginning!

Sometimes, the orchestra crowded into coaches for a distant engagement; at other times, we caught local buses or trains to less distant concert venues.

But whichever way we travelled, the excitement of performance never wore off.

One major opera was staged every year by the college, punctuated by orchestral concerts each term. Whether picking one's way through darkened orchestral pits, or walking out onto a fully lit platform, with the background hum and rustle of an expectant audience, the excitement would rise to a crescendo until the conductor raised his baton, silence fell, and the performance began.

It was then that the magic took over.

Time and place were forgotten. One was swept along in Tosca's tragedy, or thrilled by the emotional turmoil of a Brahms or a Tchaikovsky symphony. Occasionally, I felt depressed by the expertise of the older students, who were the soloists in various piano or violin concertos, but I felt sure that with ever more practice, I would achieve their standards in the end.

Those nights were wonderful!

The spell of being part of a big orchestral unit didn't break until the performance was over, and an enthusiastic audience showed their appreciation with applause.

It was at this time that Gran died.

Her passing was my first experience of the fragility of life, and the cold finality of death.

Grandfather's death had not touched me in the same way as Gran's death was to touch me.

Other than mourning his loss, and attending the funeral with the rest of the family, his life had not been closely involved with mine, because he had never lived with us.

My parents had made all the necessary arrangements, dealt with everything connected with their house, and my own life remained relatively untouched.

But Gran had been a very real person to me, woven into the fabric of my life.

She had come to live with us on the same day that Grandfather died, and for the next four years, she had always been there.

How I wished I had been kinder to her, more understanding of her own difficulties, more patient with her ramblings.

It was my great loss that I had never known her as the vibrant, capable woman she had once been.

I don't remember a time when her joints had not been swollen and mis-shapen with rheumatism, and I can see her now, sitting by the fire, rubbing Wintergreen into her aching knees, to try to relieve the pain.

In those last years, she had wanted so much to return to her own childhood home, not understanding that it lay many hundreds of miles away, across the sea.

Usually it was the neighbours, but occasionally it was the police, who would find her wandering outside as far as a mile away, and bring her back to us.

Yet again, she would tell us, it was getting late and she had been walking 'home', and she would be full of admiration for the wonderful paths that had been laid, not understanding that these new 'paths' were actually roads!

As dementia increased, her adventures became ever more alarming, and my Mother employed a lady to be her companion, during those times when the house would otherwise be empty.

Wednesday afternoons at College were reserved for sports, and were without any lectures or tutorials, so they became my 'companion' times, listening to Gran's confused recollections of the past. In her younger days, Gran must have known very real poverty.

Even though my parents had long ago bought carpets for them, when she and Grandfather had lived in their own home, Gran continued to feel the need to make "peg rugs".

These were rugs made of clothing bought at jumble sales. The material would then be cut into four-inch strips, and each strip would be hooked into a canvas backing. We had bought Gran a "Do-It-Yourself" craft kit, on how to peg your own rug, the wool being colour coded, to match the pattern stamped on the canvas.

But it was just too difficult for Gran to follow the instructions. My Dad would sit by the hour at night time, un-pegging all her mistakes, whilst I sat at the other end of the rug, re-pegging the wool into the correct pattern.

Dad had the patience of a saint!

One particular Wednesday, the companion had left at the arranged time, but I was late getting home because a bus, or maybe a train, had been late. As I walked up the path to the front door, panic hit me. The bathroom was at the front of the house, over the front door and hall, and water was cascading through the porch ceiling, running down the front door, down the steps and out onto the path!

Goodness knows why, but Gran had put the plugs into both the bath and the sink, turned on all the taps, and come downstairs to peg the rug.

Shortly after my arrival home, the ceiling fell in!

It was not long after this episode, that Gran died.

Poor, sad Gran.

Remorse is indeed a bitter companion.

After finishing college with five years of study behind me, and armed with a degree and various diplomas and certificates, I was ready to take on the world.

One of these qualifications was a teaching certificate. I had no intention of ever making use of it, as I never intended to become a teacher, but as it was possible to fit teaching lectures into my timetable without encroaching on the time needed for a performance diploma, or interfering with attendance at other lectures, it seemed a good idea to study for it, and thereby have a useful 'extra' qualification in reserve.

Little did I realise at the time, that what I thought of as a 'handy extra', was to be the most important bit of paper of all!

I looked to repeat the thrill of performance by getting work as a full-time orchestral violinist, but competition for contracts was fierce.

The best opportunities for work lay in London, home of most of the big orchestras and opera houses, and the multi-national record studios.

I found "digs" around forty miles from the city, and even though short-notice deputy work came my way, payment for it was irregular because the engagements were irregular. Only the rent demand for the bed-sitter was a constant feature of life. Some weeks, after travel expenses, there was no income left, so occasional free-lance teaching seemed a helpful choice.

After all, even a little money was better than none at all!

With subsidies from my parents when things were really bad, I stayed on in my bed-sitter, such as it was. The furniture was crawling with silverfish, and riddled with woodworm holes, but I felt that if I could just weather this financial storm, all would come right in the end.

I can see that room now!

My bed was against a window, and even the morning that found the windowsill crawling with mature woodworms ready to take flight, failed to deter me! I was making good connections in the city, and they seemed well worth keeping.

That fourth Winter, however, was a disaster. With an erratic income which had often left me without enough money for heating, and at times without sufficient food, there came one weekend which found me feeling more than usually depressed, and not very well.

Having no engagements, I packed a case and decided to go home for a couple of days.

The Inter-City train, supposed to be arriving in the early evening, ran into snow drifts and frozen points, and didn't arrive at the main-line station nearest to home until around three o'clock in the morning!

British Rail rose to the occasion, however, and everybody was eventually sent home in taxis!

Feeling by now really ill, I crept into my home without waking anyone, and went to sleep in an armchair in the sitting room. What should have been a weekend at home, turned into a month of bronchitis and pneumonia.

The miserable conclusion was inevitable - life had to change, and my flirtation with freedom and independence was over.

Dad and I drove down to London, packed all my belongings into cases and bags, the car was loaded, and we set off on the long and bitter journey home.

CHAPTER 2

And so a new chapter began, and with it, the urgent need to get some kind of regular work.

As long as I kept practising, the dexterity and skill in my fingers, only achieved after so much study and so many thousands of hours of practice, would surely not be lost.

But what was available?

Very little, it appeared, for an over-qualified musician with dreams of greatness!

The dreams were put on hold. Something would surely turn up - it was just a matter of waiting on opportunity.

Any kind of job, to fill in what I considered to be only a temporary set-back, became the most pressing need. I applied for, and was appointed, as a primary school teacher in a very deprived area of a nearby city, which was within reasonable travelling distance from home.

Work as a primary school teacher proved to be exhausting. In that first year of full-time teaching, I found no opportunity to use my practical skills, and at the end of the working day, was drained of the energy that was essential for at least four or five hours of concentrated violin practice.

However, there were opportunities for both mental and keyboard skills, and wishing to share the fun and achievement to be found in music, I set about adapting - completely re-writing would be a more appropriate description! - a Gilbert and Sullivan operetta.

The chosen victim was H.M.S. Pinafore. It was a massacre of Gilbert's fluent and clever writing, and a travesty of Sullivan's musical inspiration, but it was a good story with memorable tunes, and one which proved to be very popular with the children.

Their parents showed unexpected and tremendous skills in the costume department, my father used his artistic ability to draw the scenery, and the good ship Pinafore was afloat!

It ran for four performances, and attracted good press

coverage and reviews from the local newspapers, but this was just not what I had imagined for myself. Teaching, most definitely, had never been my chosen profession, and the misery of my own school days was not far enough behind me, to turn life in the school room into an attractive proposition.

I still played in amateur and semi-professional orchestras, and made new contacts in my own professional world. One of these led to an invitation to write both words and music for a radio documentary.

Perhaps success was to be found down this avenue which, until now, had been unexplored.

Again, after various applications and interviews for work in the world of broadcasting, the result was failure, unless I was prepared to go back to London.

Unable to take on another doubtful enterprise which, like the previous one, would perhaps end in debt and illness, I started looking for another job that offered better use for my abilities.

As in any profession, there is an underground network of contacts, and an exchange of information. Teaching is no different.

The Headmaster of a big secondary school, in what was then called a 'Social Priority Area', had seen H.M.S. Pinafore, and offered me a job in his own school, on a slightly higher salary. The barely hidden agenda behind this offer, was that another production would be mounted, improving the status of his school, and thereby enhancing his own professional status.

Although my parents did not really approve of the move, feeling that if I was to remain in teaching, I should at least move to a school with some kind of musical tradition behind it, I saw it as an opportunity to pass on to what could only be described as seriously deprived children, some of my own enjoyment in music.

The idealism of youth!

I thought of that elderly lady who had encouraged, and endured, my early efforts on the violin; I thought of all those solitary nights in the music hall, listening to symphonies and concertos, carried away to a world of beauty and glory; I thought of the sheer feast of sound that was Der Rosencavalier.

It was time to give something back, of what had been given to me. Determined in my own mind that this job would only be for two years, or three at the most, and tempted by its financial security, I accepted the offer.

The next Gilbert and Sullivan operetta was in the pipeline!

This time, the victim was to be "The Pirates of Penzance", but on a more ambitious scale than Pinafore had been, and with a much bigger cast.

Again, the parents joined in whole-heartedly. The Housecraft teacher took on responsibility for costumes and interval refreshments, the Woodwork department made scenery, the Art department painted it, and other staff became overnight experts in make-up, wigs, lighting and scene changing!

It took me the first four months at this school, writing at nights and weekends, to turn Pirates into a viable night's entertainment, and one which could be managed by the children. Gilbert and Sullivan had written their work for trained professional adults, so a good deal of the language needed simplifying, and the music needed to be brought within the range and capabilities of eleven to sixteen year olds.

After the Christmas break, with well over one hundred sheets of manuscript completed, work with the chorus and the principal singers started in earnest.

Right through the Spring and Summer terms, and on into the Winter term, every lunchtime, and every afternoon when lessons were over, a timetable of rehearsals took over, some for the chorus, some for the principals. The only person needed at every rehearsal was me which, in addition to teaching a normal timetable of lessons, and the usual end-of-term exams, plus parents nights, and staff meetings, and departmental meetings, and so much else, was an exhausting workload. But success depends on practice, and I intended the Pirates to be a success.

If it were to fail, it would not be through my fault, because I had not worked hard enough.

The Pirates exceeded all expectations!

On the opening night, towards the end of November, there were unsold tickets available for all the remaining nights. By the following day, however, word had gone around the neighbourhood that the Pirates was a show worth seeing, and every remaining ticket was sold before the end of that morning. Many people came each night even though they had no ticket, filling every last square inch of standing room in the hall, and overflowing into the corridors.

Hopes of a career as a professional violinist had quietly moved into the background during all this activity. Dreams of life in an orchestra, even as a Second rather than as a First violinist, were receding without any conscious realisation. No grand decision was taken, no heart-wrenching acknowledgement of failure was ever made.

A determined effort to maintain a regime of violin practice of at least four hours each evening, had plainly become impossible during the production of the Pirates. Four hours of practice had slipped to three, then two, or even one, until the occasional evening was missed out altogether.

There were only twenty four hours in a day, and in the war of attrition between how many hours were spent on school work, for which I was being paid, and how many hours were spent with my violin, which was a personal choice, there could only be one winner. It was useless trying to deny the truth - a career in an orchestra was not an achievable goal, and I may as well admit it. Perhaps it was time to change direction, and to become what I had promised myself I would never be - a career teacher.

With this altered perspective, the years passing, and still nothing to show for so much work, I thought of moving into the property market and perhaps buying a house of my own. It would not be easy on a single salary, but it could hardly be worse than life had been with the woodworms and the silverfish of bed-sitter land. After all, I was not a stranger to life on a limited budget. I had lived for years without sufficient heating, and considered food to be merely an unfortunate, but necessary, outlay of cash. However, with a steady job and a regular income, the main worry of paying the mortgage would be under control. To be a home-owner would give me security, it would be tax-efficient, it would be an achievement, and it would mean freedom. What had started as a stray idea became a definite possibility, and within the year it was a fact - I had my own house!

CHAPTER 3

My parents were wonderfully supportive and generous at this time - they gave me so many things from their own home to help me towards independence. Mother bought net curtains for the windows that could not be fitted from her own spare curtain stock, and Father tirelessly decorated every room , although I doubt that he had seen himself having to work so hard in his recently acquired retirement!

When it came to the garden, though, I refused all offers of help.

Having been used as a tipping site for builders rubble, clearing the land was a mammoth task, and it was work that was much too heavy for either of my parents to do.

I would attend to it myself.

If I had known at the beginning what was involved in this task, my courage must surely have failed.

Moving into the house in Spring, I had not had the advantage of seeing the problems that the rain and snow of Autumn and Winter would bring with them.

Nor had I realised how many half bricks and stones could be found in such a small patch of land!

At the end of that first Summer, I had managed to clear only half of the land that was destined to become the back garden, and the rubble extracted from it had grown into a small mountain.

From wondering where to tip so much rubble, and how on earth to remove it, it became a real blessing that I had kept it.

The garden lay under several inches of water during most of January and February, which was a major difficulty.

Frequent sessions were needed in the local library, reading about land drainage, and how to solve the problem of standing water. The only affordable solution, which by co-incidence was also the correct one, was to make several, big soakaways.

From a problem to which I had no answer, the rubble mountain became the solution. How glad I was that it had not been tipped!

I invested in a pair of heavy duty, industrial wellingtons, and with a pick axe borrowed from a neighbour, started the unenviable task of digging holes that were big enough, and deep enough, to be soakaways for Winter rain.

An occasional, regretful shadow would flit across my mind, when I thought about all the insurance premiums that had been paid in the past, insuring my fingers and hands for thousands of pounds, and then thought about the heavy work that I was now doing.

How priorities in life change!

One Saturday morning, I was digging yet again in one of the soakaway holes. I had read in the library about how to shore up the walls of deep excavations, in order to prevent them from collapsing, and possibly injuring the person who was digging.

This, I felt sure, was a word of warning to those who excavate deep roadworks, but would not apply to my own holes. In any case, I had built into one wall in each hole, five or six steps leading to the bottom of the hole.

Nothing would collapse. There was no need to worry.

One day, I stood up straight to relieve the pain in my aching back, and found with a shock that my own eye level was just below the level of the ground, and a wild idea occurred to me.

Was I digging my own grave?

Would I suffocate and die here, alone in my back garden?

Was this to be my end?

Summoning up an energy I had thought long gone, I headed for the rubble mountain and started filling the soakaway, throwing in bricks and stones with a speed and urgency that surprised even me!

At last, after weeks of labour, the soakaways were finished and some real garden planning could begin.

A winding path along one side of what was now referred to as "the garden" rather than "the tip", seemed a good idea. That once despised heap of rubble had become a valuable resource, and best of all - it was free!

My path would be made of whatever suitable pieces I could find in the rubble, but before making the path, it was more important to stabilise the bottom end of the garden, which was almost two feet lower in height than the land next door.

This difference in land levels was, of course, the explanation of why my own patch was so heavily water-logged. In heavy, or prolonged rain, the soil was washing down the slope, and the water collected and lay on my land, simply because there was nowhere for it to drain away. The second Winter in the house was to prove the effectiveness of the soakaways - the sheet of water that had been my back garden was gone, and the idea of a little path was now a definite possibility.

In a state of great optimism, Mother arrived one day with half a dozen rose trees, to plant in the projected rose border. And Dad would arrive on Saturdays, equipped with a hammer and a spirit level, to work on the path.

And so the second Summer passed.

In the cool of the night, I often went into the back garden, lit by the fitful flare of a burn-off pipe from the nearby oil refinery, to survey my handiwork.

These were treasured times of stillness and peace, and I think, also, of a deep and almost tangible happiness.

One particular Saturday, unusually free from the burden of school work, I went outside to weed what was, by now, turning into a recognisable rose garden.

And unexpectedly, I was about to read my first "Sermon in Stone".

A fast growing weed had spread its roots under one of Dad's carefully laid pieces of broken flag. Being resistant to both pulling and digging, there was no alternative other than lifting up the piece of flag, to remove the weed's roots.

Out of respect for the occasional hedgehog searching for his night's food, and for visiting birds hunting for aphids and spiders and insects, choosing chemicals either to promote the growth of plants in the garden, or to deter weeds, was never an option. The garden was a chemical free zone, and would remain that way.

I lifted the flag.

To my horror, I had uncovered a nest of ants, thousands and thousands of them, running everywhere! My initial reaction was typically human - kill them!

A second thought was to replace the flag and try not to think about it.

But what if I replaced the flag and inadvertently trapped the ants?

Or worse, suppose they got squashed but not killed, and were left injured and dying?

There were so many of them, and I had no answer.

Even to kill one of them began to seem unacceptable, and how would I choose which particular ones were to die?

Surely the life of even one ant is as important to that ant, as one human life is important to that human. And whilst there may be seriously depressed humans walking the earth, whoever heard of a suicidal ant, nursing a death wish?

After the first horrified recoil, I laid the flag aside, feeling the need for some time to think. Those few minutes turned into almost an hour, a passing interest became an absorbed fascination, and the longer I watched, the greater my perception of ants changed.

I saw the soldier ants, whose mission in life was to repel attackers, running over my shoes, and biting and stinging my hands; worker ants, already trying to repair the damage I had caused to their nest; and nurse ants carrying their precious cargo of eggs, the future of their colony.

And there I stood, a veritable Colossus, deciding their fate.

Did the Great Spirit, I wonder, look down on His creation with sorrowful heart, viewing the devastation that humans continue to

18

inflict on His planet? Is His relation to the Earth, the ant hill of human life, similar to that of me and my ants' nest? Is He watching a myriad self-absorbed lives going about their business, the majority of them without any thought or care for a greater, eternal dimension, as He holds life, and death, in His gift?

No.

The flag must remain at the side of the garden, and not a single ant must be harmed.

In this life, though, nothing is static. Whether recognised or not, whether accepted and welcomed or not, everything is constantly changing.

Nothing lasts.

And for me, change was lying only a few months ahead, waiting to ambush me, ready to bring this so newly found sense of happiness and contentment, crashing around me in pieces.

CHAPTER 4

First of all to get, and then to hold, the attention of a classroom full of Secondary age children, relying on the past success of the Pirates of Penzance was not going to be enough.

The attention span of children is notoriously short, and during rehearsals of the Pirates, it had surfaced as a vague idea that although these young people hugely enjoyed the singing and acting and costumes, and all that went with a big production, this kind of music belonged to a past age. It was, to be honest, not really their scene.

Their more immediate thoughts were about fashion, and discos, and pop music. And being a mixed school, their most frequent thoughts were about sex!

It was time for a major re-think. If one could not beat the opposition, then why not join it?

The Christmas break following the production of the Pirates of Penzance seemed, for most of the students, to have pushed its memories into a very distant past.

I was now fully occupied adapting the score of Gilbert and Sullivan's Mikado, and thinking of a possible production date of eighteen months ahead.

By Spring of that year, the manuscript score was finished, but within the school, everyone's attention was fully focused on exams. Recruiting for the Mikado would have to be postponed until the Autumn term.

By this time, however, the principal singers had left the school, enthusiasm had turned first into a passing interest, and had then evaporated completely.

It was time to put the re-think into action.

I bought a Spanish guitar and an introductory book, and began to listen to the radio stations that were popular at school.

I learned to play the guitar quite easily, as I already understood the theoretical requirements, and had strong and agile fingers through playing the violin.

A Spanish guitar proved not to be loud enough for class singing, however, so I then bought a twelve string acoustic guitar, and learned to play, and sing, hundreds of folk songs, and more hundreds of the fashionable popular songs that I so disliked.

As a change from the piano, I spent many hours during the day playing the guitar for class music lessons, and many more hours at night, learning new songs and chords.

When playing a guitar, the angle and position of both the arms and hands are obviously very different from those adopted when playing a violin.

I had noticed that my little finger was no longer responding instantly to changes of guitar chords, and for some unknown reason, it seemed to have lost much of its strength.

The pin was out of the grenade.

Over the following couple of days, an odd sensation of coldness and numbness spread across part of the back of my hand, and then for two days, the little finger was completely useless.

Thinking of the past, and of a student I had known whose life and career were ruined through too much practice on a wind instrument, which had resulted in a torn diaphragm, I presumed I had damaged a ligament or tendon in my hand, through too much playing.

Feeling slightly worried, but not unduly anxious, I booked an appointment with the local doctor.

What followed must surely stand as a classic example of how a doctor should not give information to a patient.

After a brief examination of the affected hand, which had lasted not more than a minute or two, the doctor pronounced that although a Consultant's opinion would be needed to confirm the diagnosis, there was little doubt that I had Multiple Sclerosis, and that it was a progressive illness, for which there was no cure.

With that careless, throw-away sentence, the grenade had exploded!

I was told that I would receive a letter within the next few weeks, notifying me of an appointment with a Consultant at a nearby hospital, but in the meantime, to continue with life as usual and not to worry.

Case dismissed - the doctor was ready for the next patient.

As with previous set-backs, I did what I had always done when things had gone wrong, and withdrew into silence and aloneness to absorb the shock.

It was a silence, thankfully, that was to stretch into almost twenty years.

The next day, I was back at work as usual.

The content of lessons needed an instant change, so that difficulties with playing either piano or guitar could be disguised, and my secret would be safe.

Within a fortnight, sensitivity and strength had returned to my hand, and life continued as normal.

But for me, life would never be normal again.

Seven months later, the Consultant's appointment arrived.

The Consultant was just as dismissive and as unhelpful as the G.P. had been.

After ten or fifteen minutes his parting remark, which I have never forgotten, was an instruction to make no plans for the future as I probably did not have one; and that the best I could hope for, would be five year of occasional symptoms, five years of progressive disability, and then a few more years after that. Goodbye, and send in the next person on your way out.

And that was it.

On that fateful day, I should have returned to work by lunchtime, but chose instead to do something I had never done before in my entire life - I played truant, and returned to the stillness and silence of my little house.

I needed time to think.

The unhappiness and loneliness of my own school days had been an excellent training ground for exactly this kind of situation. "A trouble shared is a trouble halved" was not an adage in which I had ever believed. Rather, I felt, sharing trouble with someone else made it a trouble doubled, not halved.

I would keep my miserable secret to myself.

Life continued as before, weeks and months passed, and I found myself more and more often, going into the back garden late at night. The oil refinery flare lit up the night sky, even though the house was just outside the two-mile blast area, and one night, when the flare was more than usually brilliant, I decided to drive down for a closer look at it.

Heard from the garden, the noise it made had only been a distant rumble, but being near to it, it was almost deafening! It lit up the whole industrial complex brighter than street lighting, although with the same orange hue.

Against those huge storage tanks, and the massive pylons, and all the associated chemical factories, the night workers were dwarfed - unimportant, insignificant figures, attending to the needs and whims of a grotesque monster, pre-occupied dots on the ant-hill of life.

Parked on a little used side road, night after night I would sit for hours, until this industrial eyesore assumed a grotesque and haunting beauty of its own.

And it was here, one Winter's night, listening to the cables vibrating in the freezing air, that I wrote my first poem, and called it 'Pylons':

Pylons marching, watching, walking,
Pylons whirring, buzzing, talking,
Pylons thinking, laughing, singing,
Pylons brooding, mourning, weeping.

Happy pylons, useful, needed,
Tall and grey, erect and handsome,
Like a web across the country,
Silhouettes against the stars,
Lighting highways, paths and bye-ways,
Bringing warmth to old and weary,
Carrying power across the nation,

People hungry, calling, begging:
Plug in! Switch on! Heat up! Cool down!
Wet it! Dry it! Boil it! Freeze it!

Weeping pylons, sad with knowledge,
Silly children, youthful, bored,
At their feet like rag dolls lying,
Hidden dangers told, ignored.
Pick up! Sweep up! Clean up! Bury!
Leave no sign to tell the tale.
Give us power, cheaper, cleaner,
Need it, want it, use, abuse it.

Tired pylons, work now over,
Arms have rusted, joints corroded,
On the scrap-heap lie, abandoned,
Silent, still, awaiting fate.
Brand new pylons, bigger, stronger,
Now feed power across the nation,
Shining, eager, light reflecting,
Carrying power, cheaper, cleaner.
People calling: "Give us power!"
Endless wanting, endless needing.

Pylons laughing, buzzing, singing,
Pylons thinking, mourning, weeping,
Watching, waiting, whirring, talking,
Silent pylons tell their story.

Although heavy industrial shapes could only ever be a poor second to the sheer perfection of a dandelion or a daisy, still, there was a strange kind of beauty to be found in them, even if only in their downright ugliness.

A sad comparison occurred to me, and it was a thought which refused to be forgotten. That refinery was essential now, but only for a short time, until something better was invented.
Unlike the refinery, however, I was not essential, and never

had been, not to any person, or any job, and I never would be.

Who would notice if I was no longer here on this earth?

Would anyone mourn for me, anyone shed a tear at my passing?

Whose life would be poorer because I was no longer a part of it?

The answer to all these questions was - no one.

Apart from the house, my life had mostly been one long catalogue of failure.

My future, whatever was left of it, was going to be one which I had no wish to live through.

It was time to draw the line, to arrange a quiet exit from this world .

I bought everything that would be necessary, and all that remained was to choose the time.

Weekends were not an option, as the risk of discovery was too great. Mondays and Fridays had to be ruled out as well as, at work, they would be added on to the weekend, and three days absence would cause comment and enquiries, and need a Sick Note.

So the chosen day, the last day of my life, would be a Tuesday.

I went back to the refinery one Monday night, to the place where I had known peace, for one last, long look.

I wanted to say goodbye to those paradoxical storage tanks, ugly and beautiful at the same time; to the buzzing cables of the electricity sub-station; to that little side road, with its overgrown grass verges and thick, wild hedges; to all those anonymous night-shift workers, attending to the needs of their monster.

And then I came home feeling totally calm, and sure of my decision.

Tuesday morning arrived, and the most important thing to remember was to behave as if everything was completely normal.

At lunchtime, I went to the Staff Room for what I believed was going to be the last time, to sit in an armchair for half an hour, and to have a cup of tea.

There was no Heavenly wind to herald the miracle that was about to happen, no angel with folded wings waiting quietly in the corner, just the usual group of teachers, exchanging un-exciting bits of news.

But all was in place, and the miracle was waiting to happen.

I was there, in that dingy, smoke-filled staff room, wrapped tight in my own dark thoughts about the events of the coming night, at the same time as the Head of Science and the laboratory technicians were there, calmly discussing the best way of killing a duckling who had hatched the previous night, in one of the Science laboratories.

Of the thirteen eggs that had been acquired for incubation, only three had hatched, and of these three, two were already dead. Through culpable ignorance, because not enough research had been done on how to care for ducklings - information I was only to find out much later - one mallard duckling had come to grief in a water dish that was too big and too deep, and without its parent's oil on its feathers to give it water-proofing, had drowned. The other duckling had hanged itself in the ill-chosen wire netting that formed the front of the hutch.

The question of: "Where, and how, to kill this sole survivor" was easily settled, and by the end of the lunch break, it had also been decided who was to carry out the deed.

But all this was none of my business.

There was nothing I wanted to do, and nothing I could do, to change anything.

My own time was now getting very near to its end.

The last class of disobedient and foul-mouthed pupils was gone, my last sun had set, and the final afternoon was over. There was no anticipation, and no regret - for the first time in months I felt totally passive, calm, detached from everyone and everything, and in control of events.

Having locked the doors of my classroom behind me, I set off down the quarter mile of corridors, to the car park.

As I came from one direction, my corridor crossed another one leading from the Science suite. The Science teacher, and I, met at the junction, to the accompaniment of plaintive little peeps, echoing down the empty, stone corridors, and coming from a large cardboard box.

A note had been circulated to all Staff during the afternoon, asking if anyone would give a home to a single duckling, but there had been no takers, so the little creature was about to meet its end.

The choice to make an exit from this world had been entirely mine, but what had this innocent creature, still less than twenty-four hours old, ever done to deserve death?

With poor grace, and irritated by such unlooked-for interference with my own plans, I agreed to take the box and its occupant, thinking that this would only put back my own plan for a few days, until I could find somewhere else for the duckling to live.

I drove home that night with my precious cargo on the passenger seat, acutely aware of my total ignorance of all wildfowl matters, annoyed that my good nature had been exploited, increasingly angry that yet again, another of my schemes had met with failure, and - the reluctant owner of a day old duckling!

CHAPTER 5

What do ducks eat?

Do ducklings eat the same food as adult ducks?

At what age do they need to swim, bearing in mind the recent tragedy at work?

Full of questions, I arrived home and took the cardboard box into the house.

Food was the highest priority, but what do ducklings actually eat?

And from where does one buy it?

Having put the car away for the night, I returned to the garage to get it out again. A quick tour of any pet shops that were still open, seemed the most important thing to do. I had to find it some food.

The second requirement, urgently, was to go for a session in the library, only this time the research would be on ducks, and not on soakaways!

Surely, there should have been the faint strains of Heavenly harmony, to herald his arrival at my home?

Perhaps a muted angelic choir in the background?

Even great arcs of lightening shooting through the clouds, and deafening claps of thunder, would not have come amiss, to greet his arrival at my house.

But there was nothing.

Nothing at all, to suggest that in bad-tempered and resentful silence, my miracle had happened.

Annoyed by the intrusion into my life, but knowing that this pathetic scrap of yellow down would need attention for at least the next couple of months, and knowing that no one else was willing to look after it, I gave up struggling, and accepted the fact that the responsibility for looking after it was going to be entirely mine.

This duckling's life now depended on my own life.

I had said nothing of what my own intentions had been for this particular week, so there was nobody who needed an explanation.

And in any case, the plan for self-destruction could still be activated in a few months time. It was a good plan, and would be just as effective whenever it was put into operation.

For me, this intrusion was nothing more than an unfortunate delay.

Although now long gone, I look back at the many photographs I took of my little duck in happier days, and reflect on how his coming into my life had so completely altered its direction.

It was only a few weeks before his golden yellow down turned pale lemon in colour, and then this, in turn, became white, with adult feathers beginning to show through.

Two or three curling feathers appeared on the tail, signifying that it was a male, and as he grew to maturity, I knew it was time to find him a permanent home.

What a minefield lay ahead!

Autumn came, and now aged five or six months old, and fully covered in pristine white plumage, I found a farm that would take him.

On asking if it would be all right if I sometimes called in to see how he was progressing, I was told that I would be welcome anytime, up to Christmas.

An alarm bell was ringing!

When living at home, I had been vegetarian for several years, but after buying my own house and being free to choose what I ate, I had become a vegan. This choice was made with only one thought in mind - I did not want to swallow pieces of dead flesh, in whatever form they were presented.

The ways of farmers, and the refined cruelty inflicted by them on farm animals were, at this time, still largely unknown to me.

(With what horror I recalled eating duck and orange sauce on my twenty-first birthday!)

Did people eat ducks at Christmas, I wondered?

I had become rather fond of the little creature, and for him to end up on a dinner plate was not something I wanted to think about.

No - a farm, any farm, was too great risk.

Still, there were other possibilities.

My next call was at a Nature Reserve. Surely they would accept him, without having any ulterior motive?

If he had been a wild mallard, he would have been accepted on the Reserve without any bother, but they refused outright to take on an Aylesbury duck.

At the time, inter-breeding with the wild duck population did not seem to me, to be a problem.

How blissful is ignorance!

I was on a steep learning-curve into the behaviour and breeding habits of ducks. There was so much to understand about breeding, and in-breeding, and inter-breeding, and selective breeding. As a result of all this research and reading, I found the answers to a lot of questions that had been bothering me: Why was he so big? And: Why did he never fly, although his wings were well developed, and he spent a lot of time flapping them?

With all this newly found knowledge, my neighbours would forthwith be denied a sight which must have given them many a laugh - I used to run up and down my piece of grass, flapping my own arms, and hoping the duck would get the idea of lifting off!

However, he was not, as I had thought, short of the idea of flight. He never achieved lift-off simply because he could not - his breeding had left him with an overweight body, designed for eating by humans, and his wings were just not strong enough, or big enough, to carry the weight of his un-natural, too-heavy body.

He was never going to fly.

Pity overcame me.

Poor creature.

He had no claws, no sting, no teeth, no poison, nothing at all with which he could defend himself, and in their greed, humans had bred out of him the one defence that was his by right - the gift of flight.

I stopped trying to find him a home.

Apart from the farmer whose dark intentions were totally unacceptable, no one would ever want him, so he was going to have to stay with me, where at least he would be safe.

The next thing to consider, then, was the quality of his life.

It would be of little use to have saved him, only for him to spend his days in a miserable prison.

The utility room in my house, now named the Duck House, was beside the garden, so I knocked a hole through the bricks, similar in size to a cat-flap, which would give him easy access into the garden.

The next consideration was swimming.

When he outgrew the kitchen sink, I used to take him up to the bathroom, where he could swim in the bath. But something bigger, and more permanent, was needed.

I bought an outdoor, fibre-glass water garden with different levels built into it - a deep end where he could up-end or dive, and a shallow end where he could preen his feathers. And along with the water garden, I bought a hose pipe to fill it, and a pump to empty it.

From being only hours old, the duck had always been mine, but now it felt like he really did belong to me, and anything I could do to make him happy, must be done.

As I sat in the garden watching him, it seemed that perhaps he, and I, were not so very unlike.

He was completely unimportant to everyone, and always had been - there were millions like him, being killed and eaten by humans every day, their lives extinguished without a second thought, their pathetic dead bodies selling for little more than coppers.

He had nothing valuable, or outstanding, to give to anyone,

any more than I had.

No one would notice when he was gone, any more than my own passing would be noticed.

The more I thought about him, the more pitiful he became.

It seemed that we were two of a kind, thrown together by fate.

Perhaps it was destiny written in the stars that, unheralded and unsung, this innocent, harmless, white-winged creature had crossed my path.

He was my angel in disguise sent, for a while, to walk beside me along life's path.

In return, I would protect and watch over him, and make his life as comfortable as possible, for however long I was blessed with his company.

And so he acquired his name - I called him Angel!

CHAPTER 6

The coming of the duck had brought into my life a new awareness of how fragile, how wonderful, how precious, is the gift of life.

It seemed not to matter any more that my career, such as it was, had reached an abrupt end. But for whatever time remained in my working life, leaving my present post was no longer an option. What should have been a two or three year stint in this depressed, and depressing school, had turned into a life sentence.

Surrounded by factories, heavy industrial units, slums and slum clearance sites, I was anchored for the duration.

Applying for a new job would mean having to fill in application forms. These forms would ask questions about health, and to answer them honestly would require giving information that I did not wish to reveal to anyone, whatever the reason.

Still, internal promotion remained a possibility, provided the MS attacks left no obvious disability behind them. It was a case of waiting hopefully, but not literally, for dead men's shoes!

So I continued at work, doing all the things that were expected of me, but the fire had gone out.

Thoughts of staging the Mikado continued to drift around at the back of my mind, but when a more senior position did become vacant, I was not appointed to it.

In the words of the Headteacher at that time: "You don't have a family, so you don't really need the extra money."

The death knell for the Mikado had sounded!

There was no longer any reason to put in endless hours of unpaid overtime, and accept all the tensions and stress that would go with a big production, if there was never going to be any reward, simply because I did not have a family.

But every cloud has a silver lining, and every setback can be turned to advantage, even though such advantage might not be apparent at the time.

My failure to gain promotion, quickly became a matter of public debate, and the bitterness of this humiliation was difficult to bear.

It was somewhat lessened, however, when I found out, quite by accident, that the parents were circulating a petition to have the job re-advertised. They felt, as I did, that this particular job should have been mine!

Whilst appreciating very much the kindness of these parents in their gesture of sympathy, I had no wish to be involved in a 'job post-mortem', so I squashed the petition as soon as I heard about it.

For me, the silver lining of this particular cloud lay in the fact that I would be seen to be justified in not staging any more big productions, without having to explain why they had stopped. It would just be assumed that I was offended, because I had not been promoted.

The real truth was that major undertakings were getting beyond my strength. The MS attacks could never be predicted, either in length or severity, so the risk of planning something to take place as far as two or three terms ahead, was just too great a risk to take.

However, for the sake of the pupils, and as an un-acknowledged thankyou to the parents for their kindness, I continued to organise events for Christmas , and Open Nights, and all the other usual school events, but there would be no more grand productions - Gilbert and Sullivan, amongst many others, could rest easy once more!

And so the terms passed.

I hurried home each evening to be with the duck, to attend to his needs, and to enjoy his company.

He had become such a lovely creature, so helpless, so reliant, so completely uncritical.

Life was running smoothly, and for the first time ever, I felt essential to the happiness of another creature, even if it was only a duck!

Sitting with him in the back garden, and watching his antics in the water garden, and his enthusiasm for hunting slugs on rainy days, led me to an interest in feeding the garden birds.

What had started out as a passing interest, became an absorbing hobby.

I read books on ornithology, memorised pictures of birds for identification purposes, and whenever time permitted, visited a wetland reserve.

In the early part of the year, the reserve was full of families who made far too much noise ever to see any wild birds. Instead, they preferred to spend their time in noisy admiration of the half-tame families of ducklings and goslings.

One visit at this time of year was enough for me.

The last thing I wanted was to be with yet more children!

And it was too sad, knowing that my Angel was condemned to a solitary, and celibate, life with me.

My visits to the reserve, therefore, were made during the autumn and winter months.

Many hours would pass when there was very little to see, but occasionally, those empty hours were rewarded when long skeins of wild ducks or geese, and some times even swans, would fill the twilight sky, returning from their feeding grounds on the coast, to spend the night in safety at the reserve. Their calls could be heard faintly in the distance, getting increasingly louder as they approached, and then a thrilling moment, if I was fortunate enough to be standing directly underneath the flight path, of hearing the beating of their wings, and feel the air disturbance on my face, as they passed overhead.

Two years elapsed in an interval of calm until one afternoon, a pupil brought a sparrow to me, who had been found grounded during lunchtime.

Over sensitive by now to the needs of any creature with wings, the plight of this little sparrow was desperate, and urgent.

As soon as I could, having found in the telephone directory the most likely source of help would be a Wildlife Rescue Centre about forty miles away, I left work for the second time, clutching a cardboard box containing a bird in trouble.

Who could have guessed that such a chance encounter with another helpless, winged creature, was going to have such a profound effect .

The sparrow's chances of survival were poor, as it had sustained a broken wing and a broken leg, probably the result of a road accident. The shock of these injuries, plus the added stress of being handled, made the Rescue Centre staff not hopeful for his chances of recovery, but they promised to do their best for him. It would be a good sign if he managed to live through the night, and they would be pleased to answer my telephone calls regarding his welfare.

Surprisingly, he did recover, and I visited him as often as time allowed, until one wonderful day, he was released.

He was just a common sparrow, completely unremarkable and of no great worth to anyone, but what a difference a few dedicated people made, in saving him from certain death, and nursing and restoring him to life!

These people had no ulterior motive for giving away their time and energy. Their commitment was to lessen the suffering of wild creatures, and in their own small way, to make the world a better place.

The requirements of work took up most of my time, but I volunteered to help at this Rescue Centre in any way that I could, whenever time permitted.

The offer of help was gratefully accepted, so first of all with guidance, and then on my own, I would run a stall at various fund-raising functions and Charity Fairs, and when not needed for this kind of work, I helped to clean out cages, feed animals and birds, or help with any other kind of work.

One wet and wind-swept Saturday, I had been out at a Charity Fair that was being held in a Victorian Town Hall. Those must have been gracious days indeed!

The Hall itself was imposing, being lofty and spacious with wide, sweeping staircases, but how unfortunate that the Fair had taken place on the first floor.

Boxes of cards and notepaper, envelopes, key rings, pens, toys and dozens of other items, having been carried up the staircase in the morning, needed to be carried down again at the close of the Fair. Those wonderful staircases rapidly lost their attraction!

On one trip, on my way up the stairs for yet another box, I passed a lady not in the first bloom of youth, resting at a landing. She was obviously another stall-holder, struggling to carry one of her own heavy boxes down the stairs, and having great difficulty with the size and weight of the box.

I offered to carry the box for her.

What an effect that small act of kindness, and a chance encounter with another cardboard box, would have in the years to come.

CHAPTER 7

Work continued, degenerating into a monotonous routine of teaching and singing, and lunchtime guitar lessons.

In time-tabled lessons, I tried so hard to awaken young minds to the beauty and interest of classical music, but I was whistling on the wind.

No one wanted to know.

The only musical interest the pupils did have, was in popular music, with its boring, mindless rhythm, its indistinguishable words, and played at a deafening volume.

Since music was not a compulsory subject for exam purposes, and offered no scope for job opportunities, the pupils saw no point in making any effort to learn anything at all.

Both the subject and I were treated with derision.

It was a depressing thought, that for all the use I was in that school, I would be better off to resign, and join the ranks of the unemployed.

But this realisation, of how entirely futile my efforts were in trying to pass on the civilising influences of music and culture, were counter-balanced in a most unexpected way, and gave purpose and direction to my continued existence.

Although not in any way that had ever been intended, within the closed community of that school, I was getting famous!

Well - a kind of fame, anyway.

I was becoming known as the problem-solver-in-chief for birds and animals in distress.

It was the sort of fame I would never have wanted, and it came with a price tag attached to it in money, time and effort, but the cost was always worth it, and would be repaid many times over.

Learning from the experience of that first encounter with Angel as a day old duckling, and then later with the injured sparrow, both of whom had had to endure long car journeys, slipping and tumbling around in cardboard boxes that were far too big for the purpose, I bought a proper bird cage to cater for any future emergencies.

It was to be one of the best investments I ever made!

From a steady trickle of occasional wild birds in trouble, of which starlings and pigeons were the most common, each Springtime brought a regular influx of baby birds and fledglings, often sparrows or blackbirds, but again, more usually starlings and pigeons.

Everything that might be needed to keep them alive, if that were possible, was stored inside the cage, and when the day was finished, I took the casualties to the Wildlife Rescue Centre.

Most of these rescues were without drama, but not always!

One morning, driving into the car park at work, I was met by a pupil shouting at me to stop, and pointing towards the sky.

If my attention had not been drawn to it, I would never have looked up at the second floor classroom windows, and still less at the gutters and roof tiles, but there it hung, an adult starling, fatally trapped!

It was too high up to see exactly what had happened, except to realise that one of its feet was well and truly caught, and that the poor bird was hanging upside down by its trapped foot.

At first, I thought it was dead, and was about to write off the incident as just a sad misfortune, when there was a sudden and desperate fluttering of wings, a strangled alarm call, and then a return to the early morning silence.

My first thought was to get the caretaker to bring some stepladders, and I hurried off to find him. Shortly afterwards, he appeared outside with some ladders, but the problem was not to be sorted out so easily.

The ladders were just not long enough - in fact, they were useless.

I had told him that the bird was trapped at the high roof level, and he had wrongly assumed that I meant the roof of the single storey classrooms, further along the building.

We went back into school, and a few minutes later, with him carrying the front end of the longest ladders I had ever seen, and me carrying the back end, we returned outside to the starling.

At this point, the caretaker told me that he never used these ladders himself, because he was terrified of heights, and as it was now half past eight and time for him to clock off, he was going home for his breakfast and I was on my own.

Well, life is nothing if not challenging!
Aware that there was almost no feeling in my bad foot, which would make climbing ladders really dangerous, but not having any better ideas, there was nothing more to do, except commend my soul to the Almighty, remind Him rather urgently that what I was about to do, was being done for one of His creatures, and with a racing heart, to start climbing.

At the beginning of the ascent, there had been only a handful of pupils watching the proceedings.
I climbed to the roof and saw what had happened to the starling.
Telephone engineers had recently updated the telephone system in the school, and they had stapled a thin cable along the length of wood between the roof tiles and the gutter. Somehow, the starling must have got its foot trapped underneath this cable, and in its efforts to pull free, had lost its balance and fallen over the edge of the gutter, thus leaving its entire body hanging upside down, suspended by its foot.
It took only a few seconds to ease the tension on the cable, free the bird, put it in the pocket of my cardigan, and begin to descend the ladder.
From start to finish, the entire rescue had taken perhaps five or ten minutes, but this had been long enough for a crowd of pupils to have collected around the bottom of the ladder.
As I very thankfully set foot again on level ground, clapping and cheering broke out - the starling, and I, were safe!
And the end of the tail?
The only injury to the bird was severe bruising to its foot, and a dislocated hip. After ten days at the Rescue Centre, it was ready for release, and would again feel the freedom and joy of

flight.

How quickly one acquires a name for knowing what to do, for being able to handle problems that could just as easily have been handled by somebody else, if they had only bothered to take the trouble.

Without any conscious thought, my entire focus on life in all its myriad, perfect forms, was changing.

There might have been thousands of other starlings in the world, like there were thousands of ants all those years ago, but there would never be this exact starling again.

And always, at the back of my mind, was the thought that suppose I had walked away those years ago, and left a cheeping baby duck in a cardboard box to take its chances, I would never have known my dear Angel, never have been rewarded with his trust, never have learned to see the miracles of life all around me.

Perhaps it was not me who had decided my fate after all, perhaps destiny had chosen an alternative fate for me.

Perhaps, instead of passing on the joys of Mozart, I was passing on something of infinitely greater value - an awareness of life itself, and the beauty and wonder of creation.

Even in the grim surroundings of slum clearance and heavy industry, there was still this beauty and wonder to be found, surviving against all the odds.

Which one would be more fantastic, I wondered - to invent the machinery to send a man to walk on the moon, or to invent the perfection of a pure white daisy growing in the crack of a pavement, or the seeds of a dandelion drifting gently on the wind?

Maybe those young people were learning about a subject that had no name. The best teacher in the world has no need for words, because the best teacher is example, and her lessons are taught in gentleness and silence.

One lunchtime, as I was sitting at my desk marking books, one of the staff and a small group of pupils arrived at my classroom door.

They came with a story about paw prints they had seen in one of the main corridors, and what animal did I think had left them?

The trouble with being given a piece of information, of course, is that once something is known, it cannot be not known.

It would always be so much easier to disregard a troublesome remark, to walk away from something which was not my business, but this piece of information was now in my head, and it could not be ignored.

I found the blood stained paw prints and followed them up staircases, down staircases, along corridors, through classrooms, and was finally rewarded by discovering a sad little dog, curled up in the corner of the well of a staircase, trying to pretend it was invisible.

He was very thin and shaking with fear, but seemed relieved more than anything else, to have been found.

I tied a piece of string around his neck and called him Sparky - I had done my first dog rescue!

Now, the real problems started.

What does one do with a rescued dog?

After many phone calls and enquiries, the situation was eventually handled to everyone's satisfaction, Sparky was officially classed as a stray, and accepted at a rescue kennel over one hundred miles away.

All I had to do now was to get him there.

But at least I had transport.

I was not being asked to do the journey without food, and to walk until the soles of my feet had worn away, and were raw and bleeding, as had happened to poor Sparky's feet.

Fortunately, dog rescues were a rare occurrence.

What spare time I had available, when it was not needed for Angel, I spent at the Wildlife Rescue Centre.

Over the years that this Centre had been operational, several ponds and small lakes had been dug out, to cater for the needs of a disparate collection of seabirds and wildfowl. These birds were healthy in every way, but could never be returned to the wild as they had all suffered some kind of permanent injury.

As my visits to the Centre became more frequent, I got to know these long-term residents - a tame goose, herring gulls and black-headed gulls with only one leg or one wing, and a swan who had been left with one and a half wings, after an argument with an overhead electricity cable, to mention but a few.

Also enjoying this sheltered life-style, there were as many as forty or fifty wild ducks, the majority of which were mallards, and amongst them all there was one, lone, pure white Aylesbury duck.

The thought was inescapable - would my dear Angel be happier with them, than he was with me?

The more often I was at the Centre, the more this thought bothered me.

After several months of worrying about it, and not reaching any definite conclusion, I talked to the Centre Manger about Angel, and asked him for his thoughts on the subject.

At this time, Angel was two or three years old, and my life was centred around him.

But was I being fair to him?

Would he be happier with his own kind, rather than with me?

After many miserable nights, I had to admit that whatever he might lose in attention from me, he might gain much more, from the companionship of other ducks.

The longer I thought about it, the more selfish it seemed to keep him.

One sad Saturday morning, I put Angel into his carrying box and drove with him, up to the Centre.

Sitting on a bench overlooking the smallest of the ponds, the Manager and I opened the box, expecting Angel to take to the water immediately, to start his new life surrounded by other ducks.

Well - isn't life just full of surprises!

Angel did not head for the water, as we had expected him to do. Nor did he join up with the other ducks, either on the pond, or on the grass verges which surrounded it.

Instead, he settled down next to my feet, underneath the bench.

Thinking he was just overwhelmed by his altered surroundings, I prepared myself to wait on the bench for an hour or two, giving him time to acclimatise, and to get used to this change in his circumstances.

The afternoon wore on, three hours became six, and dusk was falling. Whenever I left the bench, Angel was walking at my feet.

I picked him up repeatedly and floated him off on the pond, but every time I did so, he got out of the water, and was back at the bench faster than I was, hiding underneath it.

Finally, I gave up.

He was just too strongly imprinted ever to want to leave me, and my efforts to give him a different life were not going to be successful.

Being frightened was one thing, but tormenting him was not justifiable.

The Manager came to the bench and told me it was a lost cause - I had better put Angel back in his box and take him home.

What a wonderful journey that was!

I had shed so many tears at the thought of life without my little man around the house, of the loneliness and the emptiness that awaited me.

There would be no more sparrows in the Spring time, swooping down onto the back garden lawn, to collect his moulted feathers for their nests - I had the only sparrows in the country whose nests were lined with feather quilts! - and the flowers would again fall prey to the slugs, but all these miserable thoughts were banished in an instant.

The decision had been made, and not by me.

There would be no more experiments with alternative life styles - my beloved, silly little Angel was mine after all, and he was coming home for good.

CHAPTER 8

It was a tremendous relief not having to fret, and worry over, what was the best and kindest thing to do for the duck. In the end, it had been Angel himself who had made the choice, and he had chosen to be with me.

From now on, we could both relax, and enjoy our time together at home.

Life at work continued as usual, with a steady trickle of young or injured birds coming my way, all of whom ended up at the Rescue Centre.

Caring for wild birds requires not only veterinary expertise and knowledge, and suitable cages or enclosures in which to place the casualties, but it also requires instant access to many different kinds of food.

Some birds need seeds or corn, others need insectivorous food, or carnivorous food, or even live food, whilst the occasional kingfisher or sea bird needs fish.

Bird care is such a very highly specialised field, I regularly gave thanks for the Rescue Centre, where I could safely leave all my problems!

Perhaps once in a year or so, a dog would cross my path, but having made good contacts at the rescue kennels during Sparky's time, dogs were not a problem, either.

All was well until one morning, when Angel was by this time about five years old, the school secretary came to my room. She wanted to know the official procedure for dealing with a dead dog.

Never having had to deal with one before, I had no idea.

My first thought, before she telephoned for the Council Cleansing Department to come and remove the corpse, was to make sure that the dog was actually dead.

The Secretary and I met at morning break, with neither of us wanting to face what we expected to find.

Climbing over the demolition site, she saw the dog before I did, and pointed it out to me. It was lying on its side, on a heap of earth and rubbish, its mouth open and its tongue hanging out.

It certainly looked like it was dead, and by the time we saw it, it must have been lying there for at least two hours.

Feeling sure that it was dead, she left the site to return to her office, intending to telephone for the Cleansing Department.

Having learned a little about the legal status of dogs, and imagining that somewhere there must be a broken-hearted owner searching in vain for this beautiful animal, I approached the dog for a closer look, to see if was wearing a collar, and hoping that if it did have a collar, there might be some kind of identification on it.

I really did not want to do this, as I expected rigor mortis to have set in, but it was something that had to be done, so I moved nearer to the animal, and bent down to feel around its neck for any kind of collar that might be there.

The body was warm!

It was not dead!

I almost ran over the demolition rubbish and back to school, to tell the Secretary to cancel her call to the Cleansing Department, and to ask her, if she could, to find an emergency cover teacher who would sit with my class for the two lessons which remained until lunchtime.

Then I went to the canteen for a plastic beaker, and filled it with water to take to the dog.

It still had not moved, and looking back with hindsight, I feel sure that it had decided to give up on its unequal struggle for life, and had found a quiet place in which it could lie down and await death.

At some time in the past, it must have been an impressive dog - a female, long-haired German Shepherd, and obviously a pedigree animal.

I sprinkled a little of the water I had brought out with me, onto its dry tongue and into its mouth, and to my amazement, the dog moved its head a little, and tried to lick its lips.

It was not only still alive, but conscious as well.

The first thing to do, was to arrange some kind of search for its owner.

Back in school it was now lunchtime, and several of the older pupils offered to spend their break time in knocking on neighbourhood doors, to try to locate the owner. As it happened, a couple of the pupils thought that they vaguely recognised the dog, so perhaps trying to find its home would not be as hopeless as I had expected.

With the search under way, I re-filled the plastic beaker with water, and returned to the demolition site to comfort the dog.

Just before lunchtime was due to end, three fourteen year old pupils came walking up the street towards school, and heading for the demolition site which was almost opposite to the school. They were accompanied by a rather unpleasant looking, middle-aged man.

He claimed that the dog was his, and delivered a couple of well-aimed kicks at her, to make her stand up. Then he pulled a piece of old chain from out of his pocket and fastened it around her neck, turned his back on all of us, and walked away, dragging the dog behind him.

Over the next few days, like water dripping from a tap, I kept hearing snippets of information about both the man and the dog.

The man was a jailbird, with several convictions for violent behaviour towards humans. Regarding the dog, there had already been three investigations into his reported cruelty towards her, but all three prosecutions had failed because of lack of evidence.

The following week, I visited some of his neighbours myself. They all told dreadful stories of his violence and cruelty towards the dog, but were all too frightened to speak out against him, fearing reprisals.

The trouble with information, as I have already mentioned, is that once something is known, it cannot be not known.

The state of that poor animal, and the behaviour of her owner, kept coming back to haunt me.

How I wished I had not interfered.

It would have been so much better for the dog to have died alone and in peace, that day on the demolition site, than to have returned to such a dreadful owner.

I was getting to be like a dog with a bone myself!

I could not get her out of my head.

Assuming a friendly attitude, but with murder in my heart, I visited the owner twice in the following weeks, on the pretext of enquiring after the dog's health, and of offering it a new home if he no longer wanted it.

I knew the rescue kennels would accept it, if only I could persuade him to relinquish his ownership of her.

All my offers were rebuffed.

He maintained his position, and as legal ownership continued to be his, there was nothing more I could do.

But the picture of her, that first day I had seen her, being kicked until she stood up, then limping off behind her owner, stayed with me like an aching wound.

A general feeling of disenchantment with other people, at their inertia and selfishness when it came to helping a distressed animal or bird, was rapidly turning into a real dislike of the entire human race.

It was almost three months later, when the owner came into school one lunchtime, staggeringly drunk, and again dragging the dog behind him, using the same piece of rusty chain that I had seen before.

Poor animal.

The dog was having more trouble than her owner, trying to stay on her feet. Using unrepeatable language, he shouted down the corridor that he no longer wanted such a useless animal, and that if I still wanted her, I could have her. Now!

Fortunately, headteachers move jobs.

The headteacher at this time was a kind man, and a dog owner himself. He had come out of his office and onto the corridor, to investigate the commotion.

Being over six feet tall and an ex-rugby player, just his presence was enough to intimidate this nasty, drunken little criminal.

Calmly and quietly, he took hold of the dog's chain, promised that he would sort the situation out, and escorted the man off the premises.

A couple of minutes later, I had his permission to take the dog to a Vet immediately, and not to return to school for the rest of the afternoon as he, himself, would cover my sudden absence.

How that dog must have suffered.

She was in such a state that the Vet was in a mind to put her to sleep straight away.

But I thought back to a certain Rook from the previous Summer.

The Wildlife Rescue Manager had given it to me, wrapped in a piece of towel, to hold for a little while, until it died.

Several hours later, that Rook had revived, and pecked me so hard that I still have the scar!

No.

At least, this pathetic dog must be given its chance of a place in the sun, however slim that chance might be.

The Vet agreed to postpone the death sentence for one week, to see if all the injections and tablets which he prescribed would be of any help, or if she was too far gone for anything to be able to help her.

I telephoned the rescue kennels from the surgery, to arrange a convenient day on which to deliver her, but they would not accept her in her present condition.

Any treatment she was receiving from the Vet must be finished, and she needed to be physically much stronger, before undertaking the journey.

I was left with no alternative - she would have to come home with me, until she was well enough for the journey to the kennels.

But what would Angel think?

I left the surgery full of foreboding, with the dog lying on the folded-down back seat of the car, and quite unable of to think of what to do with her.

Did I know of anyone who wanted a dog, or anyone who would look after her, even for just a few weeks?

By the end of the journey home, the only definite thought in my head was that the welfare of the residents must take priority over that of any new-comers.

Considerations for Angel had to come first.

It had been obvious that the Vet thought I was chasing shadows in trying to help this dog. As he told me much later, although nothing had been said at the time, he had not expected her to survive for more than another day or two.

But the will to live is a strange thing, as I knew from first-hand experience!

When I arrived home Angel was, as always, in the kitchen waiting for me. Seeing the dog, he froze for a moment, and then without any further concern, resumed his normal routine. He went over to the door and stood in front of it, waiting for me to open it, and to go out into the garden with him.

The dog showed no interest at all, either in him, her surroundings, or in anything else. Even the offer of food elicited only slight interest.

Her mind had completely closed down, and it was to stay that way for many months ahead.

I took her into the living room, where she lay down on the fireside rug, and leaving her to be quiet and untroubled, I returned to Angel.

This first meeting of Angel and the dog had passed without incident - I felt weak with relief!

Things would probably have been very different, though, if the dog had not been so desperately ill. Her physical condition remained critical for several weeks, and she was poorly for months afterwards, but this painfully slow recovery was actually a blessing in disguise, twice over.

Firstly, it gave the two animals plenty of time to get used to each other's presence around the house, and secondly, it gave me the opportunity to read, and learn, about dogs and their behaviour.

The story of the dog's recovery is too long, and too complicated, to write it all down, here.

Suffice to say that eventually, after almost a year, she did recover.

But I never took her to the kennels.

Instead, she became my wonderful and intelligent companion for the next three and a half years.

CHAPTER 9

At this time, life seemed to be going well.

With a wry smile, I would survey my private empire with great satisfaction and contentment - I had my own little house, a delightful duck whose life I had saved and who gave me many hours of pleasure, and a wonderful dog whose mind had finally woken up, and whose devotion and loyalty were beyond question.

Perhaps I had missed my way after all - should I have been running a wayside tavern called "The Dog and Duck"?

Well, maybe not!

There is no feeling in the world that could ever compare with the satisfaction of knowing that a life had been saved, because I had bothered to care; of knowing that the world was a better place, even if it was only enhanced by the presence of one more sparrow or a single starling, because I had been in the right place, at the right time, and had bothered to care.

So many birds flew free, because of me. I would never know or recognise any of them again, and the birds owed me nothing except to be themselves, but they had been given a second chance in life, and it was me who had given it to them.

All the money in the world could not buy such a fantastic feeling of satisfaction and achievement!

And I thought of the dogs, too, re-homed and happy with new families.

Long since, these dogs would have forgotten about both me, and their bad times.

Their new families, and I, would never know or meet each other, but it did not matter.

They were dogs who had come out of the shadows, to live a peaceful life without the cruelty, or suffering, or neglect that they had known in their dark days. For me, knowing this was enough.

When I sat in the garden watching Angel busy doing 'duck things', with the dog lying peacefully beside me, and wanting nothing other than just to be there, I felt I was amongst all men, most richly blessed.

Even the MS was quiet.
There had been no big 'flare-ups' for quite a while, although failing energy and strength were an ever present reminder not to feel too optimistic

The dog needed to be taken out every few hours, day and night, because her bodily functions were never going to recover completely from the treatment she had endured during her first six years with the previous owner. As well as needing to relieve herself, her liver had been permanently damaged by the many kicks she had received, and she was often sick. .

I had been almost unbelievably lucky, to find a retired couple who were willing to take on the responsibility of caring for the dog during the hours I was at work.
Some years earlier, I had helped these people after a cat had caused mayhem in one of their bird nesting boxes.
The box had been occupied by a family of blue-tits, until a cat had staged an early morning raid on the box, killing one of the parents and several of the chicks. After this disaster, the other parent abandoned the box because of the disturbance, leaving several more chicks, still alive, inside it.
Fortunately, this couple lived in a bungalow, so it had not taken more than a few minutes for me to climb up to the box, get the five remaining chicks out, and take them to the Wildlife Rescue Centre.
Although several years had passed since this event, the couple had not forgotten the tragedy of the blue-tits and their nest box, and looking after the dog for me, during the day, was their way of saying thank you.
However, after collecting the dog each evening on my way

home from work, the night hours were all mine, and they were not without interest!

One Winter night, in the early hours of the morning, the dog and I were walking around the neighbourhood roads, the pavements slippery with frost and ice, when I took a fall.

I was no stranger to 'biting the dust', as falling is a frequent event for people who have MS, but who are still mobile.

This fall, however, was rather different from previous falls, because I had hit my head on the pavement, and was unconscious.

I had no idea how long I must have been lying there, probably not more than seconds, or maybe a minute or two, but I regained consciousness to find the dog stranding guard over me, making little whimpering noises, and energetically licking my face!

What a blessing that no one had seen me fall, and tried to help.

Having read so much about wolf behaviour, and of the affinity between dogs and their wolf ancestors, and of the loyalty of German Shepherd dogs in particular, to their owners, I doubt that the dog would have allowed anyone at all, no matter how well-intentioned they were, to come anywhere near me!

Months later, we were on another of our night walks, this time late in the evening of what had been a lovely Summer's day.

It was a route we had walked many times before - it was part of our territory, so to speak.

A group of around a dozen loud-mouthed, teenage youths had congregated at a street corner, drinking cans of beer.

My intention had been to cross the road to the other side, in order to avoid them, rather than to have to pass near to them.

They were an intimidating sight, and I was frightened.

But the dog had other ideas.

This was the route we always took, and she saw no reason to change it.

Although I had not spoken a single word, she was very aware of my fear, and her walking speed had slowed down, although its direction had not changed.

Unexpectedly, I was in quite a dilemma!

Should I pull on the lead and try to force a big, powerful dog to do something that it obviously did not want to do, thereby risking a confrontation with her?

Or should I let her proceed as she wished, risk a confrontation with this unruly mob, and hope that they would not harm us?

I need not have worried - she handled the problem herself.

The fur around her neck had been erect, ever since her walking speed had slowed down, which was a first warning.

Now, as we got nearer to the street corner, she bared her teeth, and the accompanying snarling was clearly audible.

Like morning mist in the first rays of the sun, the youths melted away into the night, and the pavement was again ours!

Good times are like bad times - with measured tread, they pass inevitably into history, and the pages in our book of life keep on turning.

Whilst they are happening, bad pages seem to turn so slowly.

With all their anger and sorrow and disappointment, their failures and misunderstandings, they are the pages that were difficult to live through.

We do not want to re-read them, and would turn them over faster, if we could.

But so it is with the good pages, as well.

We would like so much to re-read them, to re-live our scattered moments of triumph and satisfaction, experience again those times when happiness surprised us, but these pages, too, turn over into history.

All we have left are the memories.

Much as I wanted them to, I knew that my good times could not last.

Everything in life is passing. Time ticks onwards, today becomes yesterday, and yesterday ticks on into history.

How fortunate I was, to recognise the joy and contentment of these brief years, even as I lived through them.

The next emergency at work was not a bird, nor a dog, but a young cat who had managed to get itself locked into a paint store room, where it had remained undiscovered from a Thursday lunchtime until the following Tuesday afternoon.

As with so many animal crises, troubles from both staff and pupils now, routinely, ended up with me.

Although admitting to a limited knowledge of animal first-aid skills, I regularly disclaimed any expertise in knowing precisely what to do, pointing out that veterinary surgeons were the qualified people, that it was they who should be consulted, and that it was going to cost money to do this.

Even the Wildlife Rescue Centre did not come free.

But no one took any notice.

As long as it was I who organised the help and rescue, the fact that it was my time, and my money, being spent on their problem, seemed not to matter.

But if I refused to help, well then, nobody did anything.

"That's life, and it's very cruel" was a common remark, or "Nature, red in tooth and claw" was another frequently heard platitude.

Such remarks are undeniably true, but are really only an excuse for inaction, a cloak to justify selfishness.

And they were comments that were particularly in evidence, if doing something was obviously going to cost money, or time, and very probably both.

Well - no matter.

My time was my own, and what better way could it be spent, than in lessening the suffering of an animal in distress, and perhaps even saving its life.

And money?

Money was of use only if it was spent on something that was either wanted or needed, to improve the quality of life for another.

To pay for all the surgery and the drugs that were needed by the dog, it had been necessary to take out a bank loan.

But what was money anyway, other than bits of coloured paper with pictures on them!

As long as there was enough to pay the mortgage, and service the debt repayments, I considered myself the richest person in the world, richer even than Croesus!

I would go on helping creatures in trouble, whatever others thought of me, although I knew by now that I was regarded as both a harmless fanatic, and an eccentric fool.

Somebody had to do something to help this cat, and yet again, it was going to have to be me.

CHAPTER 10

Birds and other wild creatures were catered for at the Wildlife Rescue Centre, and dogs could be accommodated at the rescue kennels.

But cats?

What was I to do about a cat?

And one who was clearly ill, served only to heighten the problem.

A Victorian Town Hall with majestic sweeping staircases was in my head.

And cardboard boxes were there as well.

I was being haunted by cardboard boxes!

After many telephone calls, I managed to contact that lady from so many years back.

Astonishingly, she remembered me, and she remembered the staircase, and the cardboard box, and Yes, she was still running a cat shelter!

After telling her the story of the cat, and explaining that because of my own animals at home, there was very little that I, personally, could do for the cat, she promised to make room for it, and we arranged for me to take it to her that afternoon.

Another first - a rescued cat!

In its desperation for food and water during its time in the paint store, the cat had been licking paint from around the lids of used cans.

As well as being severely dehydrated, the ingested paint had caused internal damage.

After a lot of veterinary attention, and weeks of after-care, the cat was to make a full recovery, and lived for the next sixteen years with one of the shelter's workers, before finally succumbing to old age.

Meanwhile, life at work was getting really stressful.

In common with many other schools at this time, and in our case aggravated by the slum clearance with which we were surrounded, numbers on the admissions register to the school were falling rapidly.

Over the space of only a couple of years, numbers had dropped so dramatically that the school was no longer viable.

The local authority's answer was to merge the school with another half empty school, about three miles away.

For the first eighteen months of the merger, pupils would continue to attend whichever of the two schools they had previously attended, but the staff would have to commute between the two sites.

For most of us, the situation was crazy!

There were days on which I started the day at one site, and during that day, had to commute two or three times to the other site.

Both sets of staff resented this enforced amalgamation and the waste of time that was involved with it, and the pupils on both sites were not slow to exploit the situation.

At last, those eighteen months ended, and the school was based on one site. But life was not as it had been before all the upheaval.

The difficulties had brought out the worst in the staff, many of whom feared for their jobs and were busy 'empire-building', and it brought out the worst in the pupils as well, who got together in gangs and regularly fought each other.

In such an unhappy atmosphere, where teachers were tired out, worried and miserable, and often barely civil to each other, it was inevitable that the criminal element in both schools would assert itself.

In times past, although this element had always been there, it had been kept under reasonable control because the teachers had known a great deal about the pupils' background, and about their family history. In the changed circumstances, however, many teachers were leaving for other jobs, and new faces were appearing in the staff room, whilst those who could, applied for early retirement.

How I wished that I could go, as well!

But neither a new job, nor early retirement, were avenues that were open to me, so it was better not even to think about them.

With such a big turn-over in staff, the criminals in the school were in the ascendancy.

Glue-sniffing was rife, and most of the 'young turks' carried some kind of concealed weapon.

One day, at afternoon registration, the atmosphere in my classroom was more than usually tense.

But I had learned better than to ask questions about anything, so made no comment.

Although divided amongst each other, these budding criminals presented a united front, a veritable wall of silence, when it came to giving away information, so asking questions would be a waste of time, anyway.

In the hope of not precipitating outright hostility, my policy had always been one of staying quiet, and saying nothing.

However, even this none-aggressive, none-intrusive policy did not always work.

That afternoon, I got a major fright, when a six-inch knife went whistling past my face, missing me by only a couple of inches.

No useful purpose could be served by reacting to the incident, so I continued doing registration, then picked up the knife in silence, and left it on a window-sill.

For the following few minutes, there was a somewhat subdued hush, then normality returned as if the event had never happened.

Things might very easily have turned ugly, but the situation had successfully been de-fused, and confrontation was avoided.

But what had I done to trigger such violence?

Did someone really hate me enough to want to kill me?

It was a sobering thought.

I could think of little else that afternoon, other than how much I wanted to go home, to be with my Angel, to sit beside my dog.

The three of us - Angel, the dog, and I - understood each other so well. I knew that I could rely on their trust and loyalty completely, whatever human beings thought of me.

Several days later, I heard from a pupil that this incident had had nothing to do with me, after all.

It had just been the continuation of a lunchtime fight between feuding gang factions, with one faction demonstrating its bravado to the other.

There was a certain grim satisfaction, in reflecting on the thought that if that knife had been thrown by someone who really had wanted to kill me, then it would have done so.

The knife had been thrown wide of the mark, deliberately.

As well as giving me a fright, though, this incident had given me something else - it altered my focus on the job.

I had never wanted, nor intended, to be a teacher in the first place.

The best years of my life were disappearing, spent in working as hard as I knew how, trying to pass on some appreciation and knowledge of my subject to the next generation.

Even though no one was taking any heed at present, and my efforts were meeting with less and less success, I had persisted in the hope that perhaps I was laying foundations for the future, when someone would remember a little of what they had heard in their school days, and walk into a new world of sound and beauty and inspiration, even as I had done.

Out of so many hundreds, I had always held on to the hope that surely, there must be some receptive minds amongst them.

Maybe it would only be one, but for the sake of even that single one, I had to keep on trying.

At some point in the future, a point that I would never know about, perhaps strains of Allegri's wonderful "Miserere" would be recollected, and pictures of the Sistine Chapel? Would Mozart's 40th symphony, or Samuel Barber's "Adagio", speak to another broken spirit, as they had once spoken to mine?

In some strange way, although that knife had not killed me physically, it had killed what little optimism I had left; it had killed my stubborn hope for the education of these young minds.

Nothing was outwardly different, lessons and exams continued, but I had admitted defeat in an un-equal battle.

I no longer cared.

And so the terms passed, and to help me live through them, I worked out how many years, and how many months, were left until the mortgage ended on the house. Then I worked out how much I was paid each month, each week, each day, each minute.

On days when I felt utterly miserable, I would take note of the minutes as they ticked passed, and imagine a small army of gnomes running into the building society where my mortgage was held, with each gnome carrying a little bag of money, with my name on it!

But life is never static, everything changes.

After those six years of drunken violence and ill treatment from her first owner, the dog was never going to make old bones.

One of the first things I had done when she had become mine, was to buy her a grave at a dog cemetery in a lovely part of the country, many miles away from where I lived, expecting that it would not be too long before it was occupied.

At the time, I had thought that even though her life had been spent in an industrial slum, deprived of everything that should have been hers by right, at least she would spend her eternity surrounded by beauty, with birds to sing to her, and wild flowers growing over her.

In those early days, thoughts about her grave had been my only source of comfort through many a dark night, spent dozing in an armchair beside her, my hand resting on her head, willing her to get better.

Her sleep was fitful, and she whined and whimpered as she re-lived her past life over and over again, in what must have been truly terrible dreams.

Often, I would whisper her name until she would awaken, terrified and trembling, and I would talk to her, and sing American-Indian chants and lullabies to her, until she had calmed down, and was re-assured that the past really was the past.

And eventually, she had got better - snatched from the jaws of eternity at the very last minute - and I was to be blessed with her company for the next three years.

But now she was slowing down, and our parting was immanent, if I had but known it.

We continued to go out on our many walks, but rather than she leading the way with me following, the order was reversed, and it was I who led the way, and she who followed.

Those times when she must have been feeling really poorly, she would stop walking and just stand still, waiting for me to turn round and head for home.

On days when it was raining, her lovely face would still lift to the sky as she smelled the wet earth, and the refreshed grass, and the newly washed leaves.

Her spirit was still radiant, her eyes still shining with the same dark intelligence, but her strength was slowly ebbing away.

One Sunday, a mellow and bright October day, we were out walking when she collapsed.

Unable to carry her, as she was a big dog and now weighed around seven or eight stones, I took off my coat and manoevered it underneath her, then dragged the coat, with her lying on it, back home.

The Vet was at the house within the hour, but all he could do was to make her more comfortable.

He had no drugs to make her young again.

That was to be our last night together.

She died peacefully at home the next day, lying on her favourite fireside rug, and I was glad that the last voice she ever heard was mine, and the last touch she ever felt was my hand, gently stroking her.

So many times, I had tried to imagine this moment, had tried to steel myself for the grief of parting, but the best imagination in the world cannot be sufficient preparation for the reality of death.

I was devastated.

The following day, a Monday, I drove down to the cemetery with her body wrapped up in the sleeping bag which had always been hers, and she was laid to rest.

With her death, part of me had died, as well.

CHAPTER 11

That sad October was over.

The days had passed, minutes becoming hours, days turning to nights, and only the sadness of memories remained.

Thoughts of the dog were with me all the time, of the good times and the bad times that she and I had lived through together, of watching her mind slowly awakening from its nightmare of cruelty, of how we had begun to understand each other, of walking together in the rain.

Having held the best staff attendance at work for the previous two years, I felt no compunction in having taken two days off work when she died. It was little enough to mark her passing.

After an initial interest at work when I had first taken possession of the dog, no one had ever bothered to enquire after her welfare, and I had never bothered to tell anyone.

The awfulness of death, the misery of grief, the searing edge of finality, everything subsides, but the mourning still goes on.

Like a ship, holed on the rocks below its waterline, grievously wounded but still afloat, so also was I, continuing the daily routine of work, but damaged beyond repair.

Spending time in the staff room, other than when attendance at various meetings was compulsory, had never appealed to me very much. Listening to stories about babies and children, of errant husbands and wives, or about the latest outing to some fashionable club or restaurant, was of minimal interest.

Being vegan, teetotal, and single, there was nothing I could contribute to the general conversation, that would be of interest to anyone.

But after the dog was gone, so was my tolerance. There was no idle chatter I wanted to listen to, and nothing at all that I wanted to share with anyone.

Visits to the staff room stopped completely.

As ever, my refuge in absorbing life's body-blows was in silence.

I was a 'wallpaper person', a living shadow, frozen in misery.

Christmas came, and went, and the year turned.

But my Angel was still with me, uncritical and undemanding, just being himself.

As long as he was there, I had time to get used to the idea that one day he, too, would be gone.

Thoughts of life without him were not to be entertained. I felt unable to handle them, believing that burdens are only laid on backs that are broad enough to bear them, and mine, quite definitely, was not broad enough to bear any more burdens.

There was some time left with him yet.

But time was inexorably moving on.

Only five months later, one dark night in February, my darling Angel took flight to eternity.

All his life, because of his breeding, he had never been able to fly.

I laid him to rest in the garden of a very dear friend, high up in the hills, where the wind would blow over him, and he would hear the call of the wild.

In death, his spirit would feel the air lifting him, and the wind beneath his wings, and he would know the joys and the freedom of flight, joys that had been denied to him here on earth.

And now, I was utterly alone.

I had been blessed for almost nine years with Angel's gentle company.

Rescued by his sudden arrival, so many years ago, from my own consuming death wish, I felt that my own life had to continue if, for no other reason, then as a tribute to his own.

In more whimsical moments, I had thought of him as my own, personal miracle. No one, least of all me, would ever have believed in a Guardian Angel in any recognisable human form, even if it had materialised beside me and spoken to me.

Over the years, looking at Angel's folded wings, at his

dazzling whiteness, at his gentleness, at his lack of any defence mechanisms, at his complete absence of aggression, I had somehow endowed him with the spirit of an angel.

He had become my own, dedicated, Guardian Angel, sent to me in a form that I could accept, and at a time when I had needed him the most.

Night times at home were empty and silent without him. I was engulfed in feelings that I knew only too well from the past - feelings of pointlessness, of weariness with life, of wanting to be gone from this world.

And now I was abandoned here on the earth, to go on existing without the two creatures who had given any real sense of purpose to my life.

But my Angel had bequeathed me something more lasting than just memories of him.

My inheritance was to know that somewhere, even if it would only be for one, as he had been a single one, there were other suffering creatures adrift in the world who needed help, who needed to share my roof space, who deserved some time in the sun.

Acquiring another duck was out of the question, even if one came my way.

Any future wildfowl casualties would go to the Wildlife Rescue Centre, to lead a more natural life with others of their own kind.

Another dog, too, was out of the question. Walking was getting to be something that I avoided whenever possible - I was failing, and I knew it.

This was a waiting time.

I was looking forward to whatever future I had, spent in a job I neither wanted nor liked, in order to earn money that would be spent on maintaining an empty house which no longer served any useful purpose.

But it was to be short-lived waiting time!

I had stayed in occasional contact with the people at the cat shelter, partly in order to hear news on the progress of the rescued cat from the paint-store at work, and partly because the lady from the shelter and I, two isolated people, had struck up a friendship.

One evening in late May, only weeks after my beloved Angel had died, the Manager of the cat shelter telephoned me. She was inundated with homeless cats, pregnant cats, young cats, old cats, adult cats with kittens, sick cats, injured cats, in fact, cats of every kind, and in every possible circumstance.

Their only common factor was that they were all unwanted, and all homeless.

Could I possibly look after any cats for her, even taking just one would be of help?

Angel had thrown me a life-line from eternity!

As I listened to the conversation, I could see that its conclusion was going to be inevitable.

The previous evening, bad news had arrived at the shelter, and things were in a desperate state.

One of the ladies who looked after the shelter's over-spill, had left for work the day before, as usual, and died very suddenly only a few hours later. At the time, there had been nine cats staying with her, and whilst seven of them had been found emergency accommodation elsewhere, there was a major problem with the last two cats.

A new chapter was about to begin - another learning curve was ahead!

I had never owned a cat and knew very little about them, but a couple of days later, two middle-aged cats had found a new home!

CHAPTER 12

When I went to collect the cats, I was bringing them into what I thought was going to be long-term foster care, and would only last until a permanent home could be found for them. As with dogs, so it is with cats - people always seem to want puppies or kittens, and are not much interested in mature animals.

Undeniably, baby and very young animals do have the huge attraction of youth on their side - they are "cute" and "cuddley", and a safe novelty to keep children amused.

Even if these same children were to annoy or torment the new arrival, the teeth of a puppy or kitten will not have grown to the point where they would cause serious damage, and its jaws will not be strong enough to deliver a proper bite.

In a young animal, as in a young child, the ancient predator-prey instincts are all present, but hidden well below the veneer of innocence and inexperience.

Within the space of a year or two, how things will have changed for both the animal and the human!

But unlike the human baby, whose increasing age enhances its status, the same cannot be said of animals.

The older the animal is, the less becomes its appeal, and the longer the time it will take, to find it a new home.

And so the first cats came to live with me. They were well into middle age, unwanted and homeless.

With amazing imagination, the ginger and white one had acquired the name of Ginger, whilst the black one with two white feet was called Blackie!

The following years saw the transformation of my house into a home for destitute cats!

From the small beginning of just two cats, who were not with me long before their category was up-graded from 'foster care' to 'resident', as they were never going to be offered a new home, the number of requests for help, for cats in distress, steadily increased.

As this never ending procession of feline casualties continued unabated, I became more knowledgeable about the ways of cats, more skilled in understanding their needs, and more competent in nursing their injuries and illnesses.

More than a thousand cats were to cross the threshold of my front door during the next twelve years and happily, most of them did, eventually, get a new home.

If those cats could only have talked, what stories they would have told!

There were the straightforward cases, such as those of some elderly, much loved cat, whose owner had died without making any proper arrangements for the care of their companion animal, in the event of their own demise.

And what is the point in any of us hoping that a visit from the Grim Reaper can be avoided - it can't!

But thinking about it, and being prepared for it, is only common sense, and will neither hasten, nor delay, the appointed hour.

There were cases of cats who had run into trouble whilst enjoying a night - or a day - on the tiles. These cats had usually ended up in vicious fights through trespassing on some other cat's territory, or had simply got themselves lost through chasing a lady, and straying too far from their own, familiar surroundings.

The majority of these cats could so easily have avoided trouble, if their owners had bothered to get them neutered.

The benefits of neutering also applied to the many cats who were pregnant, or those who were trying to survive in the open whilst caring for their kittens, newly arrived in a hostile world.

If only the owners had got them neutered.

And then there were all the road accidents, often causing

fractures to the leg, or jaw, or pelvis, amongst a variety of other injuries.

But undoubtedly, the most upsetting cases were those of deliberate cruelty.

I saw things which no one should ever have to see, living proof of humans at their most perverted and cruel, and I would be left aghast at the excesses of my own species.

Amongst all these victims of human carelessness, neglect, and cruelty, there was always a sprinkling of those who were just too old, or too injured, for anyone ever to want them.

These sad creatures found refuge and safety at my house - it was a place where they could spend the rest of their days in peace.

As cats are not sociable animals, and having regard for their need for territory, I re-organised the back garden, and had it enclosed with wire netting.

Ginger and Blackie now had their own, exclusive, part of the house, and were free to use the garden without the stress of having to assert their territorial rights.

Other cats, and later on, kittens as well, came and went, but these two old cats seemed to be fixtures, and I no longer thought of new homes for them.

Other casualties - fortunately not too many - who were destined for permanent residence with me, were dispersed throughout the rest of the house.

Amongst the early tragedies was a cat I named Pixie.

She was well into her later years, in very poor condition, and badly underweight.

But what a beauty she must have been in the past - a big, all black Persian, with green eyes!

She had spent three days and two nights, marooned on a frenetic traffic island, until a sympathetic motorist had taken pity on her plight and rescued her.

Getting professional help and advice was her immediate need, and I returned from the Vet with an impressive array of drugs.

Weeks passed, and Pixie responded well to the various medications. She was gaining weight, her gentle nature was asserting itself, and everything was going well for her.

It was only to be eleven weeks later that she had a massive convulsion and died.

Had so much effort and money been worth it, for only eleven weeks?

I had hoped for at least a year or two for her, a time of tranquillity in her sunset years, but eleven weeks!

It seemed so unfair.

That night, I sat and wept for her, but life still went on.

There were so many hungry mouths to feed, so many litter trays to clean out, so much bedding to wash, spending time weeping for one who was gone beyond all help, was a luxury for which there was simply no time.

The memory of Pixie's few weeks with me, and the anger and incomprehension I had felt at her passing, stayed buried in my sub-conscious for many years ahead.

Although never welcome, Death was a not infrequent visitor at my house during those cat years, and on the rare occasions that I successfully cheated him, the only word to describe that feeling was elation!

One chilly Autumn day, a cat I named Dusky had climbed into the engine of a car, probably looking for a warm and safe place to get some sleep.

Unfortunately, the car which she had chosen belonged to people from many miles away, who were out on a day trip.

Her presence was not discovered until the people arrived back home, and the car was being put away for the night.

Where it had been parked, on some flags in front of the house, the driver noticed a stain on the ground.

It was blood!

Another drama was in full swing, another crisis needed instant attention!

Having travelled about forty miles in the engine of a moving car, Dusky was in deep shock and badly injured.

The Vet held out very little hope for her, but he was willing to treat her injuries and make her more comfortable, if that was what I wanted, after which I could take her home, although he felt it would all be a waste if time and money.

Still, it was his time for which he would be well paid, and it was my money that would be paying for it.

My role was not that of an executioner, so I chose that he would attend to her, and I would bring her home anyway.

At least she would die somewhere that was more comfortable than on an operating room table.

Normally, I had always accepted professional advice regarding the best course of action to be taken in difficult circumstances, so why I chose to disregard such advice on this particular occasion, remains a complete mystery to me.

Dusky came home, swathed in bandages and more dead than alive.

During the night, I checked every hour or two, to make sure that she was still breathing, although there was nothing that I could have done even if she had stopped breathing, and the following morning, we returned to the surgery for some of the dressings to be changed, and more injections.

Gradually, our trips became less frequent - Dusky was out of danger and on the road to recovery.

A case of tragedy turning into triumph before my very eyes!

Four months later, Dusky was completely recovered, and went to a new home

All was running smoothly and I was content, rescuing cats who had fallen on hard times, and giving back to them the chance of a happier future.

Then the first discordant note sounded, quietly at first, but becoming noisier and more insistent, until it was a note that demanded to be heard and obeyed.

This was to happen not at home, but at work.

CHAPTER 13

The Age of Technology had arrived.

Polite invitations were being issued for all staff to attend lectures and courses on the applications, and uses, of computers in schools.

Most of the staff, as I did, gave these invitations nothing more than a cursory glance, and then forgot about them. At the end of a day's work, there were better things to do with whatever time was available, than to spend it in attending voluntary lectures, on a subject that was of minimal interest.

But nobody was allowed to forget these notices for too long.

Polite invitations gave way to instructions, and then became compulsory orders.

Whether we liked it or not, and most of the staff did not, we were all going to be made computer literate!

For me, this was nothing less than a disaster.

So many skills were disappearing, and are now more or less completely gone, in favour of the omni-present computer screen and its mouse.

I had vivid memories of the many peaceful hours of my youth, sitting beside an inter-city express train railway line, recording the names and numbers of steam locomotives.

To occupy the hours, I embroidered endless pillow cases and table cloths, learning how to do chain stitch, and satin stitch, and many other stitches, watching something slowly taking shape beneath my fingers.

It was an interest that lasted through the years, leading on to the more complicated realms of Largatera embroidery and drawn-thread work.

It would be true to say that in all my years of teaching, I never came across a single pupil who showed the slightest interest in embroidery, or crochet work, or even knitting.

And this was not for any lack of effort on my part, in trying to share my interests.

The discipline of careful sewing, and the patience needed to follow patterns, had all been suffocated by the computer, where results were immediate.

The 'mouse' had taken over, and I was out of step with 'progress'.

Along with the disappearance of the steam engine, embroidery, knitting, home-cooking, and the many other humble, manual skills that gave such a tremendous sense of achievement, so also were disappearing the accomplishments of the musician.

Years spent in learning how to play a piano, had given way to just weeks learning how to play an electric keyboard.

Instead of two hands and ten fingers, the new requirement was for one hand, and maybe only one finger!

And it was not even necessary to learn how to read music notation.

As long as the melody had been memorised, and could be picked out with one finger, an array of buttons could be pressed to select whatever combination of rhythms and harmonies was wanted, and the keyboard automatically did the rest.

How I resented those modern keyboards!

And yet another new headteacher was appointed to the school.

His predecessor had suffered a serious heart attack, probably brought on by stress and over-work, and had abruptly disappeared from the scene.

It was my very bad luck that this new headteacher decided that music should now be offered as an examination subject.

I had been at that school for approaching twenty years, and this was the very first time that music had been given its rightful recognition as a suitable examination subject for school leavers, but it was recognition that, for me, had come too late.

Alongside the revolution in the mechanics of making music,

and in order to accommodate it, the content of the National Curriculum had undergone a radical change as well.

Compared with the curriculum content of my own years at school, music was now almost a different subject!

In addition to a weekly two-hour lecture on computers, attendance at which was compulsory for all staff, I knew that I also needed help from the twice weekly, one-hour voluntary lectures on the national curriculum, prescribed for my own subject.

I had always believed that actually listening to music, rather than just hearing it, and understanding how it fitted into its historical background and that of its composer, was of major importance.

It was an approach that was now confined to the refuse-bin of history. The new emphasis was on making one's own music.

Music is always noise, but the corollary is not true - noise, most definitely, is not always music!

Instead of understanding notation, and appreciating the subtlety and inspiration of the great composers of the past, the 'new think' was to write down one's own, invented music as a computer graph.

High or low on the graph indicated volume, colours ranging from orange to grey indicated pitch, and various shade of blue and green were for speed and rhythm.

Not only was I amazingly poor at learning the 'computer speak' needed to produce this new method of notation, but I scorned the electric keyboard with its 'quick fix' results.

And perhaps worst of all, I was completely without interest or enthusiasm in trying to acquire any of these new skills

Was it for this purpose that I had spent all those years learning about music, and so many thousands of hours in the practice necessary to achieve physical mastery of the violin and the piano?

I was in the entirely ridiculous position of no longer understanding my own subject, and of trying to teach something in which I saw no point.

Whilst despising electric keyboards, I was beginning to hate computers, the new curriculum, and all things modern!

How true is the saying, that "Old dogs can't learn new tricks"! I felt old and battered, marooned in an alien and stressful world, and without any spirit to learn these new skills, or to replace my old ideas with modern ones.

I was well out of my depth, and I knew it.

The world was marching on, but it had left me far behind.

CHAPTER 14

Not only was the world marching on - so, also, was the MS.

When having to walk along the numerous corridors at work, which I now did only when it was absolutely necessary, I had worked out little ways of helping myself.

Rather than use the centre part of the corridor, which is where most people would walk, I kept to the margins, so that there was a wall beside me, and I could lean against it and use it as a support, rather than risk falling over.

Likewise with staircases - if there had not been a banister rail beside them which I could pull on, to help my bad foot up to the next step, I doubt I would have been able to manage them at all.

Occasionally, another teacher, or a pupil, would make some comment, wondering what was the matter, and from having prided myself all my life on speaking the truth, I was rather shocked to find out how fluent I was becoming at telling lies!

Lessons in the classroom needed some compromises as well. Instead of standing unaided to play the guitar, I now stood in front of my desk but half sitting on it. Increasingly, though, I opted to play the piano, so that I could sit down properly.

Attacks came and went, and it was very much a case of two steps back, but often only one forwards. Every time the illness flared up, a limited recovery would follow, but each attack always left behind it, just a little bit more damage.

"Death by a thousand cuts" was a comparison that often occurred to me.

These days, feeling tired, when not feeling totally exhausted, was a permanent state. Tiredness is a state if mind, I told myself, and blamed the National Curriculum and those wretched computers.

But really, I knew it was more than that.

To make life a little easier, I told the lady at the cat shelter that, as well as getting too old, I was now getting too busy at work, to take in any more cats.

It made me so sad, thinking of all the information that had been stored up over those twelve years, of all the specialised equipment I had bought, and all the trays, the food dishes, and the bedding that I had accumulated, but it was work that must now be carried out by people younger than me.

I was just too old, and too tired, to go on.

More than anything, though, I felt sad for the cats.

The young cats, and the kittens, would most probably survive and get new homes, but what would happen to the old ones?

Who would find space for the old ones, like Pixie? Or for the injured ones, like Dusky, who needed months, rather then weeks, of nursing and care?

The flow of in-coming cats stopped, and only the residents were left.

My hope for these, was that I would be able to manage physically, for as long as they were with me - I hoped that I would be able to 'see them out'.

And for the most part, that was how it happened.

One of the resident cats, who had belonged to an elderly lady until she died, had come to me aged fifteen years, having lost his tail and fractured his pelvis in a road accident some years previously. He spent six years with me, before his heart gave up.

Another one, known to be sixteen years old, was unwanted for no reason, other than that he had grown old, and a kitten was now preferred. He stayed with me for another four years, before dying with kidney failure.

And Blackie and Ginger, who had started the whole cat adventure, and had been with me for eleven years, died within weeks of each other.

They had been together for so long, that when Blackie was put to sleep with inoperable cancer, Ginger seemed not to want to carry on without him.

He gave no warning signs, other than being less interested in his food, and without any fuss or bother, I found Ginger one morning, lying cold and stiff in his litter tray.

One by one, the residents were departing for the Great Garden In The Sky, and the house was getting less busy.

Unfortunately, the same could not be said of work.

Here, life was getting increasingly out of control.

As well as an over-load of computer information, much of which I barely understood, I was drowning in what could only be described as a deluge of paper work, generated by the National Curriculum.

Reading and absorbing it all, then having to write and submit schemes of work for it, not only occupied the holidays, but kept me up, night after night, until the early hours of the morning.

Trying to do all this extra work, whilst keeping up with the demands of normal lessons, lesson schemes, marking books, examinations, end-of-term reports, probation reports, parents nights, staff meetings, department meetings, and all the other things as well, was desperate.

I had a small cut on one of my fingers, which had somehow become infected. Although very painful for a while, I thought of Gran's old country remedies, and as often as I could, sat with the bad finger soaking in water that was as hot as I could tolerate.

After several days, the pain suddenly decreased and the finger burst.

Not to worry, I thought, having a septic finger was something that could happen to anyone.

It had barely healed up when the same pain returned, only this time in one of my thumb nails.

Gran's remedy had worked for a finger, so why not for a thumb?

Actually, it was quite restful, sitting quietly soaking my poorly thumb and looking out at the garden, thinking back to the Dog and Duck days.

But to be honest, I knew that I was being rather stupid.

If I had been one of my own animals, I would have gone to the Vet for antibiotics, as these were obviously what was needed.

A visit to the doctor, at this time, would have saved me a lot of pain, as well.

But I had never been a 'pill-popper' - it was only a matter of enduring the pain, until the body had had enough time to heal itself.

And a lot of pain later, it did. The thumb swelled up, then burst, and then began to heal over.

I now had one completely recovered finger, and an almost recovered thumb, when one night, I was awakened with sharp pain in my hand.

Was this more of the same, I wondered, or was it MS in a form that I did not recognise?

Well, time would tell, so I went to work as usual.

The pain stayed with me all day, and that night I went to bed earlier than usual which, in the event, turned out to have been a good idea.

At least I had caught a few hours of sleep before pain jerked me awake in the small hours of the night, and its intensity kept me awake until morning.

At the time when I should have been setting off for work, I decided that enough was enough, and I had better get some antibiotics.

By this time, both wrist and elbow were stiff and swollen, and my shoulder was beginning to stiffen, as well.

Of more serious concern, however, was an angry scarlet line, running up the length of my forearm.

Reluctantly, I made an appointment to see the doctor.

It was well over ten years since my last visit, and judging from his previous performance, I expected nothing from this taciturn man, other than a one minute conversation, and a scribbled prescription.

During the half hour which followed, the doctor gave me a sick note to cover two weeks absence from work, and floated the idea that if I wanted to give up work altogether, there were ways that this could be arranged without any reference being made to the fact that I had MS.

An impossible dream had suddenly become possible!

I could hardly believe that what I had wanted, and dreamed of, for so long, might actually happen.

But it did!

On my return to work, I said nothing to anyone.

I had no great friends amongst the staff, so if I left work I would not be missed by any of them.

And the pupils would not miss me, either. They would easily find someone else to torment, with their raucous behaviour and their foul-mouthed language.

At last, I was on my way out!

CHAPTER 15

Unobtrusively, I started to sort out at work the accumulated paperwork of a lifetime, bringing home everything that was for disposal, so that even the caretaker and cleaners would not be alerted to my departure, by the sudden and unaccustomed enthusiasm for tidiness and order.

I would have expected this interval to be a period of great excitement, even elation, but it was not.

On the contrary, it was utterly depressing.

So many hopeful hours of work had been spent in writing a five-year syllabus, when I had first been appointed to this job. So many more hours of mind-bending work had then been spent in researching and writing for the National Curriculum, thinking through its aims and objectives, and planning its schemes of work.

And it had all been for nothing.

All the records and audio tapes of the great classical composers , which I had collected, and looked after, and treasured for all these years, would be discarded in favour of CDs, or more likely, would be discarded and not replaced at all.

All the prints of the great artists spanning the last thousand years, would quickly be defaced by the pupils, and then thrown out as just so much more waste paper.

With deliberate and measured intention, I was throwing away my life.

It could hardly have been called a successful life, though, so why worry?

At least I was escaping from a world to which I did not belong, and to which, in truth, I never really had belonged.

But it was depressing and upsetting, just the same.

My departure was fixed for the middle of one week in January. The doctor would give me a sick note for a couple of weeks, to be followed by further sick notes, and I would resign officially at the end of July.

All went according to plan.
I was still fairly mobile for almost a year, following my departure from work.
Having been self employed for quite a few years before going into teaching, and then leaving earlier than I had intended, made my financial position somewhat precarious, but mortgage repayments on the house would soon be finished, and when that happened, my worries would be over.

Worries about the MS were increasing, however, as the illness began to assert itself. I started to use a walking stick, which was helpful for a little while, until a walking frame became necessary.

Thoughts of what would happen to the remaining resident cats, if I became more significantly disabled suddenly, were uppermost in my mind.
There were only two cats left with me now, and these two needed some concentrated consideration regarding their future.
Both of them were cruelty cases, both were handicapped and not suitable for new homes, and neither of them were more than six or seven years old.

Good fortune smiled on me!
Through various 'cat friends', I found a dedicated, private sanctuary which was willing to accept them.
Set in more than a hundred acres of woodland and fields, and being over a mile from the nearest road, this sanctuary was absolutely ideal.
Autumn was ending, and one cool day in November, it was time for the last cats to leave me.
After all the activity of arranging transport, and packing their medication, and their beds and dishes and toys, it was with a heavy heart that I watched the van drive away.
Another page had turned, another chapter was closed.

There was no future to which I could look forward, except one of declining health and increasing disability. Nor was there a past on which I could reflect, and savour at length its triumphs, however small they had been.

The house was eerie in its silence, with not a single animal to disturb the stillness.

Having been alone in my head since childhood, and physically alone after student days were over, I was well used to my own company.

Now, for the first time, I was not only alone, but lonely as well.

I spent a great deal of time, looking at photographs of my dear, sweet Angel who had saved my life, and of my beloved dog, who would have given her own life, if she had thought that by doing so, she could have saved mine.

And I thought about the cats, too. How difficult it had been, to relinquish responsibility for their care to some unknown person.

Unlike dogs, a cat's loyalty is not so much to its owner, as to its territory.

I knew that I was going to miss the cats, a lot more than they were ever going to miss me.

The edge had been taken off the sadness, though, by thinking of the wonderful life which now lay ahead for them.

With the best intentions in the world, I could never have given them enough space in which to claim their own territory, or the kind of freedom that the sanctuary could offer them.

Nor, if they had remained with me, would they ever have been able to breathe such pure air, or to have 'cat adventures' in meadows and woodland.

CHAPTER 16

Looking back at this time, it was an interlude of stillness, a time which widened the vistas of thought, a time of beginning to learn how to slacken one's grip on life, with all its attendant possessions and trappings, a time of learning to confront and accept the inevitable, a time of beginning to learn how to let go.

Anger had been with me since the first, dismissive appointment with that uncaring and self-important doctor, when I had learned of my fate.

Until now, anger with this doctor, who had made me feel like an animal must feel as it stands in the slaughterhouse waiting to die, anger at his off-hand and uncaring diagnosis, which offered no help or encouragement of any kind, had been an ever-present backdrop to the daily task of living.

And a greater anger burned - anger at the cruelty and neglect suffered by so many animals.

The culture of cruelty endured by farm animals is widespread, and it is justified by farmers and supermarkets alike, who hide behind the excuse of needing to keep the shops full of cheap food.

Their real reason is the maximisation of their profits.

And all the while, people consider the cost of food in terms of money, rather than in its true cost, in terms of animal suffering and deprivation.

They turn their faces away, and prefer to remain ignorant of the shocking reality of pig breeding units, of sheds crammed with tens of thousands of battery hens and broiler hens, of dairy farms full of cows who are kept in a constant state of lactation, with the inevitable, but unwanted, 'by-products' of calves.

By deliberately remaining in a state of ignorance, shoppers feel free to buy the sanitised end-products of the farms, with a relatively clear conscience.

And I was angry with the people around me.

Populations of wild animals maintain their own stability, as I knew from the Wildlife Rescue Centre. But who was responsible for the constant stream of domestic 'pet' animals, unwanted, abandoned, and abused?

Why is it, that every animal rescue shelter throughout the country is always full, with waiting lists of ever more animals needing a space?

Why are so many millions of cats, dogs, rabbits, hamsters, guinea pigs, gerbils, and so many more, born into a world where they are neither needed nor wanted, to live out their lives in squalor and misery?

Compared with the price of a holiday, or a car, or fashion clothing, or tobacco and alcohol, to have an animal neutered is not expensive.

Yet so many people seem just too selfish to bother over their animal's welfare. Neutering is dis-regarded, and treatment for fleas and worms is ignored.

Whether through the farming practices of intensive breeding, or the ignorance and carelessness of 'pet' owners, it is always the animals, and not the people, who end up suffering.

I had done my best for the wild creatures around me. Not even once had I refused to answer a rescue call, and there had been many times when it would have been so easy to turn away.

As a volunteer worker, I was under no obligation to respond to calls for help, to go and pick up battered or sick hedgehogs, injured wild birds, or distressed cats or dogs.

Many times, it had not been convenient to answer the calls, but pity for these damaged creatures had always won the day.

No matter how many more starlings or pigeons or sparrows flew around, no matter how many more cats or dogs walked the earth, each one was an individual life, and there would never be this, particular life, ever again.

These suffering creatures had no hands other than mine to help them, no voice other than mine to plead for them, no car other than mine to carry them, when they could no longer walk or fly.

In all honesty, I had tried my best, but it was a best that was just not good enough.   Shelters and Rescue Centres remained over-flowing.

And I was angry, too, over the loss of my chosen career - my life should have been spent as a musician, not as a teacher.

And a deep-woven thread running through all this anger was that, no matter how hard I tried, I could not change anything.

I had done my best, trying to teach pupils whose ears were closed to the glories of music, and whose eyes were shut to the beauty of art, and the wonder of the Creation which surrounded them.

Despite my best efforts, I had made little, if any, impression on any of them.

I had done my best to protest against the excessive and refined cruelty of the farming industry, and the involvement of the retail trade in this industry, by living a committed vegan life.

But it was a protest so insignificant in size, as to be less noticeable than a single grain of sand on a beach.

And there was nothing I could do to stop the relentless progress of MS.

It was a terrible anger, an anger that never left me, hovering in the distance like the dark and threatening horizon before a storm.

And now, with too much time to think, the storm clouds of anger at my own impotence to change or alter anything, were billowing across the skyline of my life.

Like great flashes of lightening streaking through black clouds, unpredictable and devastating in their power, a terrible despair would sometimes engulf me.

Was this what life was really all about, being weighed on weighted scales that always tipped to the side of death?

When other people were at the height of their careers, jetting off on foreign holidays, and looking forward to a still fairly distant retirement, I sat alone in an empty house, looking forward to nothing except an increasing reliance on other people, to a time when I would have to endure the indignity of strangers washing me, feeding me, combing my hair, changing my clothes.

How I dreaded what lay ahead!
How I hoped to die, before enough time would have passed for the future to have become the present!

Had I really learned nothing from seeing so many hurt and dying animals, from watching the spirit of life leaving its mortal home?

I imagined a tiny circle drawn around every life-spirit, every bird, every animal, every human.
The next circle, a wider one but from the same central point, enclosed all the earth.
Wider was the next circle, enclosing not only our Earth, but the sun, the moon, the stars, the whole solar system.
And wider again was the circle holding the entire galaxy, and the uncountable millions more of deep space.
And then I imagined a square, encompassing all these concentric circles, and outside the square was the power that had brought them all into existence in the first place, a power so mighty that it was unknown and unknowable.
Was this power, this Creator whom we call God, observing individually every single circle drawn around each life-spirit, whether it be an ant, a bird, an animal, a human, a whole world?

These were the thoughts of empty days, and dark, sleepless nights.

Occasionally, some cat owner whom I had known in the past, would telephone me for advice about a feline problem they were experiencing, but my usefulness in actually being able to do anything that would be of any practical help, was over.

Or so I thought.

Covering a period of twelve or eighteen months, one such owner had telephoned me several times, telling me about a distressed cat who came from a house close to where she herself lived.

When first observed, this half-ginger and half-white cat was dirty and hungry, but did not appear to be injured in any way.

As its owner was known, the cat had legal status as the owner's property so, other than giving it food, no more could be done for it.

When the cat did a disappearing act, weeks at a time and sometimes several months would pass, before I would get another telephone call, telling me that "Fred" had been seen again and was, as usual, dirty, thin and very hungry.

There seemed no end to the wilful neglect by people who should have known better, towards their supposed 'companion' animals, whom they professed to love.

After almost two years of this "watching brief" over Fred, the next news I heard was that he had appeared again, looking more than usually thin, without any appetite, his fur blood-stained, and dried blood encrusting a gash which ran from behind one of his ears, across the back of his neck, and ended near the top of his leg.

His would-be rescuer visited the owner with offers of free veterinary care, free food, a new home, everything possible, but all offers were brusquely refused

There was nothing that anyone could do to help poor Fred.

CHAPTER 17

Two days later, just after six o'clock in the morning, I was awakened by the ringing of the telephone.

More news about Fred!

His owner had been taken into hospital during the night, and as the partner had left home some years previously, the children had gone into the care of the Social Services.

This was bad news for all concerned, but not for Fred!

For him, it was the best thing in the world that could have happened!

Within a few hours of the telephone call, Fred was with a Vet, receiving intensive treatment for the next three days, after which it was his rescuer's intention to take him to her own home, where she could care for him properly.

But things never work out quite as intended - her own cats seriously objected to poor Fred's presence amongst them.

Time for a re-think!

On the understanding that feeding and litter trays would be attended to each morning and evening by the rescuer, and that she would also carry out all the subsequent visits to the Vet that Fred was going to need, he would be welcome to stay with me.

Fred's sojourn with me was to be rather longer than had been anticipated, as his owner died whilst in hospital, and Fred himself needed veterinary care for over six weeks.

With the death of his owner, Fred was now both homeless, and ownerless.

But when he eventually did recover good health, what would be his future?

Did he even have a future?

It could not be with me, although I would dearly have loved to have kept him.

It could not be with his rescuer, as the welfare of her resident cats took precedence over Fred's welfare.

There seemed no solution to the problem, other than to board Fred in a cattery, and hope that on the off-chance, someone would see him, and offer him a new home.

It was time to do some serious thinking!

I often telephoned the sanctuary where my own two cats had gone, and they were having a wonderful time.

If it was good enough for my own, I thought, then it was good enough for Fred.

But the problem was transport, and it looked as if it would be insurmountable.

I could think of no-one who would be willing to give up a whole day, and undertake a round trip of over five hundred miles, just for the sake of one cat.

Surely, there must be someone .....somewhere.....

Then inspiration struck!

If people without cars overcame their difficulties by using a taxi, then why not get a taxi for Fred?

Four months after his arrival at my house, Fred travelled to the sanctuary in a super, private-hire taxi.

This was 'arriving in style' in a big way!

I wondered what people must have thought, seeing an apparently empty taxi when it stopped at traffic lights or motorway services, but occupied by a single cat, enthroned on the back seat!

Still, what other people thought was up to them - I had found Fred a fantastic new home, guaranteed for the rest of his life.

I could ask for nothing more.

Once Fred had gone, time hung heavy.

During his stay with me, I had come alive again.

I had been like a spider at the centre of its web, industriously spinning and weaving, repairing torn threads, exploring the possibilities of how to extend the web!

There had been so many things to arrange, and appointments to make, and then dozens of telephone calls to confirm or cancel them.

Every appointment for Fred with the Vet, had needed a time to be fixed with the receptionist - fortunately, a way-back friend from the time when I had been a frequent visitor to the surgery myself - and then the appointment had needed to be confirmed with his rescuer, to make sure that it was still convenient for her to keep it.

As regards transport, the complications had been horrendous!

Remembering the advertisement, I had "let my fingers do the walking" through various telephone directories, until I had found a private-hire taxi company that was in the first place, willing to accept an unaccompanied animal as a passenger, then if they had a driver who would undertake to carry an animal on such a long journey, and then to fix a meeting date at my house that was convenient for Fred to be collected, and also for his rescuer to be present, in order to wish him goodbye.

Apart from imagining the hole in my bank account after so many telephone calls, I felt like I had one flat ear!

Those who laughed the last, and the longest, would be the telephone company shareholders, gleefully gathering in mega-dividends from their shares!

But none of them could have been as pleased as I was, thinking of Fred and his new home.

After Fred's departure to pastures new, the house was silent again, and there was time to think of other things.

Walking from one room to another was getting ever more difficult, and whilst not wanting to bid the Devil 'Good Morning' until I met him, and much as I resisted the thought of a wheelchair, it was time to think about acquiring one.

Giving in to disability is not an easy thing for anyone to do, and I fought every inch of the way before admitting to even the smallest defeat.

Two years previously, I had had my bed brought downstairs.

Falling when already downstairs was one thing, but the risk of falling on the staircase itself, had become just too big a risk to take any more.

Sleeping downstairs made me feel very sad, partly because, though tacit, it was a public admission to visitors that the staircase was no longer possible.

But mainly it caused me sadness because it vividly brought back thoughts of my lovely dog.

At first, the dog had gone upstairs to sleep at the side of my bed.

When she could no longer do this, I had brought my bed downstairs, so that I could sleep beside her, whilst she slept on the sofa.

Times when she thought I would not notice, she used to get onto my bed and go to sleep on it herself!

Now, I was finding that getting into bed at all, was becoming impossible.

I could sit on the edge of the bed, then by falling backwards I could lie across the bed, but my leg muscles had no strength and my feet remained planted on the floor, heavy and useless.

Not sleeping in a bed was another defeat, and a big one.

The bed was replaced and nights, as well as days. were now spent in a riser/recliner armchair.

There were some advantages to this arrangement - after all, every cloud has its silver lining! - and having remote controls for the television, video, and hi-fi system, made them instantly available for twenty four hours, every day!

But having a wheelchair did not necessarily mean that it had to be used. It could just be regarded as back-up, a kind of safety net, for when life was really difficult.

So I went ahead and filled up the forms, fighting my way through red tape, and ordering taxis for attending the necessary hospital appointments.

Months later, a shiny, new, state-of-the-art powered wheelchair arrived. (One refrains from calling it an electric chair!!)

I parked it in the hallway, hoping to put off for as long as I could, the miserable day when it would have to be used.

That day was to come a lot sooner than was expected.

I had another fall, which left me with my feet and ankles twisted awkwardly underneath me. Try as I might, I could not manage to free them from beneath my own weight.

I lay in the hall for nearly four hours, before finally admitting to myself that for the first time ever, I was completely helpless, and needed to call out the emergency services.

How thankful I was then, to have the hated wheelchair waiting for me!

Life on wheels was not as dreadful as I had thought it was going to be, and surprisingly, it was not without its moments of humour.

I had always liked dodgem cars at fairgrounds, and being in the chair was rather like having an unending dodgem car ride, but without any other cars to get in the way, and without any rubber fenders to absorb the shock of crashes.

The furniture took   quite a beating!

There were excellent controls on the chair, instantly responsive to the slightest touch.

One day, having switched on the television early, so as not to miss a programme that I particularly wanted to watch, I caught the last few minutes of a competition for downhill skiing.

Ski-ing was something that I had never done in my life. Nor had I ever been white water rafting. Or mountain climbing. Or parachute jumping. Or anything, really.

Suddenly, I wanted to feel the wind in my face, and to move faster than the minimum speed of four miles an hour, at which the wheelchair was set.

Picking the longest and straightest route in the house, which was the length of the hallway, I turned the dial on the chair to its maximum speed of eight miles an hour, and directed the lever forwards.

My Angel was busy again!

How I did not catapult myself straight through the front door and out onto the road, is still a mystery!

It had been quite a thrilling few seconds, but it was not a thrill I wanted to repeat!

I turned the chair speed back to the minimum, and settled for watching the television.

Something else that I had not often done, because until now, there had rarely been enough time, was to read the local free newspaper, which was delivered weekly.

Mostly, I just glanced at the front page headlines, then put it unopened, in the waste paper re-cycling bin.

One week, feeling at a loose end, I read the entire paper, even the pages of miniscule print, where the local council gives notice of highway repairs, and any new parking restrictions in the nearby town.

Buried in these columns of fine print, there were also details of Planning Applications to the local council, for home extensions or structural improvements to existing properties, and details of applications for new buildings.

One of these applications came as a complete shock, and was to occupy my time and thoughts for the next two years.

CHAPTER 18

There it was, buried in print so small that an earwig using a magnifying glass would have had difficulty in trying to read it, an application for Planning Permission to build sixty houses on the field directly behind my house!

This land had been a playing field, used by a school built about fifty years ago, but following recent government re-organisation, the school was no longer needed, and not in use.

It was a big field, with three sides occupied by buildings, whilst the fourth side ran without interruption to where the oil refinery had once stood.

There were numerous objections to the loss of the field for yet another housing estate, in what was already a densely populated area, but the field was irretrievably lost - the Council had sold it to a builder for a great deal of money.

The builder would obviously intend to recoup his financial outlay on the land, and make huge profits for himself at the same time, by building houses on the field as soon as possible.

There was just no point in objecting to the housing estate - the field was sold and already lost.

As these things usually are, everything would have been agreed months previously, behind closed doors, with a nod and a wink and a handshake, and all would be over, bar the shouting.

In return for 'sweeteners', the Council's officials in the Planning Department would have taken great care that they left behind them no evidence of any meetings between themselves and the builder.

As long as the officials kept their side of the bargain, and made sure that the builder got permission to build his houses waved through the Planning Committee, all would be well.

Any objections to the plans would be discussed at Planning

Committee meetings, at which these same officials would be present, to be consulted in their role of 'experts', at which tine they would recommend that the plans be passed.

Sitting on the Planning Committee would be a selection of elected councillors, most of whom would know little, or nothing, of the area concerned, and whose paid service to the Council was, for them, little more than a one-night-a-month hobby.

Notice would be given of the objections, and the councillors would call in their so-called 'experts' for further opinion.

The opportunity for corruption is obvious.

The builder 'sweetens' the official, who then appears in his guise of 'expert', and recommends that the Plans are passed. The councillors defer to their 'experts', the Plans are given the rubber stamp of approval, and everyone is satisfied.

Objecting to houses being built on the field was a lost cause.

In one corner of the field, however, occupying perhaps a quarter of an acre, were five mature, forest trees.

Other trees had been planted near them, during the years when the school had been in use, and these younger trees were now thirty, or more, years old.

But the forest trees were in a different league.

There were two oaks, two beeches, and one horse-chestnut, and they belonged to a bygone age when, according to old maps, the entire area had been a forest.

What is now a big town three miles away had, until the nineteenth century, been only a small cluster of cottages along the edges of an ancient Roman road, surrounded by this huge forest.

These mature trees, already several centuries old, must once have been part of that ancient forest, and still had centuries of life ahead.

I knew I could not stop the field from being built on, but perhaps I could save these few, old trees?

Was there any chance of a reprieve for them?

The game was worth the candle - I would try!

My courage most assuredly would have failed, if I had had any idea of the minefield that lay ahead!

But those lovely trees had no one to speak for them so, naively believing in democracy, and integrity, and honour, I decided to protest on their behalf.

I wrote to the person named on one of the Council's letters of notification as 'the person dealing with this matter', to enquire after the fate of the trees.

My only answer was a postcard of acknowledgement.

Other letters followed, enquiring after the fate of the trees, but apart from further postcards of acknowledgment, no letter was ever answered. It seemed that either the staff at the Town Hall was chronically overworked, which I doubted, or it was totally lacking in both courtesy and good manners.

Aware that builders do not wait around - time being money - I was getting steadily more concerned over the trees, and increasingly angry at the deafening silence from the Town Hall.

The Oxford dictionary defines the word "public" as 'the people as a whole', and its definition of the word "servant" as 'a person who has undertaken to carry out the orders if an employer'.

I felt that this so-called public servant - the "person dealing with this matter", whom I will now refer to as Bloggs', although this is obviously not his real name - should have replied to my letters.

After all, I was a member of the public, one of 'the people as a whole', and Bloggs was indirectly employed by me. It was my taxes that paid his salary, his pension, and everything connected with his job.

And if for no other reason, then out of common courtesy, Bloggs should have replied to my letters.

I had been angry over so many things, for so many, many

years.

It was the anger of a moorland peat fire.

There was very little, if anything, to betray its presence on the surface, but beneath the ground, the fire was steadily smouldering and burning, never going out.

I was angry with the loss of my musician's career, and the thankless and frustrating job which had taken its place.

I was angry with the food industry, whose treatment of animals is so horrific, and causes so much suffering.

I was angry with the wilful ignorance and selfishness, and on occasion, the downright cruelty, of so many owners of companion animals.

And now I was getting very angry indeed with Bloggs.

I could not solve the evils of the world, but I was determined that I would have some kind of an answer to my letters about the trees.

The pent-up anger of thirty years had found its focus at last, and it was on Bloggs!

Like it or not, he was going to reply to my letters.

When the dog had been alive, we had walked past those lovely old trees hundreds of times.

I had taken photographs of them, singly and in groups, for no reason other than that they were magnificent to behold.

I had looked at them rimed in the frost of Winter, or heavy and glistening with snow.

I had rejoiced when Spring time had burst their buds, and they seemed covered in a shower of green confetti, a time when they were alive with blue-tit parents, hunting caterpillars for their young.

The dog and I had found coolness beneath them on hot Summer nights, when I had tried to count the number of bats using them as a Summer roost.

And in the Autumn winds, we had chased together after their falling leaves, and watched the squirrels busily searching for acorns and beech mast.

An entire year was passed since I had first seen that seemingly insignificant little notice, of the application for planning permission.

It had been an entire year of writing letters to Bloggs, which he had steadfastly refused to answer; an entire year of thinking about, and worrying over, the trees.

My anger had changed - the slow-burning, underground peat fire was now burning above ground, and it was out of control.

I was like a volcano, growing ever bigger with its own suppressed pressure.

Although the trees remained untouched, and no builders' cabins yet disfigured the field, the lack of any action was un-nerving.

And meanwhile, the continuing and determined silence from the Town Hall had turned my anger into fury.

Towards the end of that Winter, and after fourteen months of writing letters to someone who refused to answer even one of them, an idea occurred to me.

Were my letters left unanswered not, after all, because Bloggs was lazy and ignorant, but because my early suspicions were correct, and he really had been 'sweetened'?

Had he been bought and paid for, and his refusal to answer letters was because he simply dared not commit himself to paper?

The longer I thought about it, the more likely it seemed.

Very well.

Even if I had been in a position to look for it, trying to find evidence of bribery and corruption would have been an almost impossible task.

Any traces would have been well hidden, as their success depends on secrecy.

I would turn the spotlight of publicity directly onto Bloggs, his secret corruption would be made public, and maybe this would provoke a reaction from him!

Within the week, I had written to Bloggs's superior, enquiring about the trees.

Like my letters to Bloggs, however, this letter was not answered either - another 'sweetened' public servant?

I also wrote to the Council's Chief Executive Officer, attaching copies of my many unanswered letters, and wondering if anything could be done to elicit some kind of response to them?

Then I wrote to the local Member of Parliament, who proved to be both sympathetic and helpful. Bloggs probably filed my letters in his waste paper bin, but he would not dare to ignore a letter from a Member of Parliament.

As the electorate is often encouraged by government to take a more active role in politics, I decided to do just that - I wrote to every Westminster department that I could think of, who might have even the slightest interest in saving the trees.

As I knew from experience, it is of no use to save an animal's life unless plans are in place for its long-term future.

Likewise, there would be no use in saving the trees, supposing that I actually could save them, unless I could find somebody who would accept responsibility for their long-term care.

The next port-of-call had to be a letter to the National Forest.

Then I wrote to the local Councillors, in whose Ward the trees and the field were situated, and also to every individual Councillor who sat on the Planning Committee.

After checking that it is legally possible to amend plans retrospectively, even after they have received Planning Permission, I suggested in these letters that the design of the proposed housing estate could be altered quite easily, omitting the quarter acre at the corner of the field, where the five mature trees stood.

These forest giants should not be felled because of, amongst other reasons, their value as a public amenity, their crucial role in wildlife conservation, and their tremendous value in pollution control.

(During my research, I had been amazed to discover that in the space of just a single day, one mature beech tree, apart from absorbing impressive amounts of carbon dioxide, releases back into the air as much oxygen as one person requires for their entire lifetime!)

At last, answers started to arrive.

Other than that from the local Member of Parliament, all Westminster letters were passed to Regional Offices who, in turn, with much politico-speak and weasel-words, referred them back to the local Council.

I could recognise a brick wall when I met one!

The National Forest would be delighted to include the tees in their overall plans for the area, and would be happy to accept responsibility for their care, but this would be subject to the agreement of the Council.

Another dead-end!

Of the thirteen members who sat on the Planning Committee, not a single one had the courtesy even to acknowledge receipt of my letter.

Of all the Ward Councillors to whom I had written, only one bothered to reply, pointing out that my own house had been built on land that had once been a field.

As this is true, at some time in the past, for every house that has ever been built, it was hardly a helpful reply!

A letter also arrived from the Council's Chief Executive Officer, telling me that Bloggs would shortly be replying to my letters!

When it came, Bloggs's letter was curt, giving as little

information as possible, but saying that a survey had revealed that one oak tree in particular, showed signs of disease, with the implication that all the trees were diseased, but that this one was more diseased than the others.

His information was based on a tree survey commissioned by the builder - hardly what could be called an impartial survey! - and I thought that this information was, in any case, not true.

However, if it was, as I suspected, a downright lie, I needed proof of the lie.

My next letter was to an international firm of Arboricultural Consultants, requesting an urgent survey and assessment of the trees, with particular attention being paid to the health of the five forest giants.

Although commissioning this independent survey had cost me a considerable amount of money, it was money well spent.

Only two weeks later, I had proof of the lie - all the trees were healthy!

The 'signs of disease' on one of the oak trees, referred to in the builder's survey, were merely scars on its trunk, left behind by damage caused about a century ago.

If necessary, the consultant would be pleased to testify in court as an expert witness, to defend his judgment.

It was this consultant's professional recommendation that all the trees, both young and mature, were in a good state of health, and 'worthy of retention' in the planning of a housing estate.

My next letter was to an Ombudsman, giving a brief summary of events to date, and signaling my intention to proceed with an Appeal against the Planning decision, and possibly, further legal action.

The Ombudsman wrote back, arranging to meet me two days later, and to meet Bloggs on the afternoon of the same day.

Although so little notice was given of these meetings, it was more than enough for Bloggs.

Telephone lines must have been busy, and within twenty four hours of receiving his letter from the Ombudsman, notifying him of the intended visit to discuss the status of the trees, all the trees were felled!

The Ombudsman kept the appointment with me the following day, but now there was nothing to say.
The trees were gone, and could never be re-instated.
Bloggs and his builder-friend had won the day.

I was sick to my soul and incandescent with rage, but there was nobody at whom I could shout, nobody to whom I could write letters, and in any case, what would be the purpose?
The day was lost, the trees were felled.

Thinking back to past years, to a time when depression and sadness had weighed heavy on my spirit and threatened to engulf me, I had unexpectedly found comfort in writing a poem about the oil refinery pylons.
Perhaps there could be a release for my misery in writing a poem about the trees?
They had been so utterly lovely in life, and so needlessly and viciously destroyed.
That which had taken centuries to grow, had taken but a few, brief hours to kill.

CHAPTER 19

Unable to sleep, thoughts of Bloggs and his despicable, shameful behaviour occupied the long hours of the night.

I could not forget the sight of those great trees, once mighty in their strength, lying on the ground in dismembered, scattered fragments.

I was tormented, wondering if there was anything more that I could have done, or anyone else to whom I could have written, who might have been able to save them.

The pen was not mightier than the sword, after all!

Still, in their own way, well-chosen words can wound as deeply as the sharpest of swords.

I decided to write a poem especially for Bloggs and his boss, and dedicate it to them. In it, I poured out my contempt and scorn for their disgraceful behaviour, and for their wanton destruction of the trees.

This poem, written in temper and slanderous in content, was completely worthless as literature, but it led me towards kinder thoughts - to reflecting on the trees, and on the beauty that had once been theirs.

How privileged I had been, to have had the opportunity to appreciate them in all their splendour.

From "The Watcher":

"................Elevated and strong,
Boughs that once were a spreading canopy,
Gifted to all who sort for shelter.
Branches that bent in greeting to the wind,
Or rustled and murmured in a Summer breeze,
Lie broken and still in death.
Great arms outstretched,
Fractured hands on the sodden earth,
Grasping fingers reaching skyward in despair,
Rain-tears trickling, glistening,
Down patterned, delicate bark......".

Does retribution await those who destroy the lovely things of this world, those who wilfully, by their actions, make this world a poorer place?

Many years ago, Chief Seattle, a wise old Indian from the American plains, taught his people that:
"All things are connected.
Whatever befalls the earth, befalls the sons of earth."
Does punishment await those who deliberately mis-treat the Earth, and exploit the lesser beings of this world, the animals?

I recalled the words of William Blake, read many years ago, and forgotten for so long:
"To see a world in a grain of sand,
And a heaven in a wild flower."

Do the words of St Francis of Assisi, written hundreds of years ago, awaken the voice of conscience in anyone, today:
" Not to hurt or harm our humble brethren is our first duty to them, but to stop there is not enough.
We have a higher mission - to be of service to them whenever they require it."

Was Aristotle right, when he wrote more than two thousand years ago:
"Until men stop killing the animals, they will not stop killing each other."

Calling across the centuries of history, there seems always to have been a lone voice, trying to awaken men to the fragility of the earth.
But it has been a call left unanswered.
Insensitivity to the world around us increases. Refusal to believe in the one-ness of creation is rampant, and a denial of the right to life in any of its forms, other than our own, is widespread.
Blind to the world in a grain of sand, we are blind, also, to the widespread suffering we inflict on the lesser beings of the world.
By refusing to acknowledge the suffering, we become

complicit in passively accepting it, and then in actively causing it.

Thoughts came into my mind of Bodger, a big white rabbit whom I had rescued many years ago. She had been kept with two smaller rabbits, in a garden not far from my own. It was only due to a neighbour that I had heard about the plight of these rabbits, after their owner had moved house and abandoned them, leaving them locked up in their separate hutches.

Already, the two smaller ones were dead, and Bodger was only barely alive, but with care and attention she recovered her health, and I was graced with her company for many years.

My thoughts meander, thinking about the fate of rabbits in general.

One such rabbit was Bodger, an over-sized white freak, who should never have existed in the first place.

Rabbits have evolved to live underground, in a complex social hierarchy, not to be kept in isolation, in a hutch at the bottom of a garden.

But they are eaten as food, chased or shot for sport, poisoned as pests, and millions die every year in vivisection laboratories.

From failing to be of service to our humble brethren, we hurt and harm them at every step of the way.

There is not a single species left on the earth that, in one way or another, has not been the loser in its encounter with Man.

And what of ourselves?

Acquiescence to the killing of animals is perhaps only a preparation for the killing of our own kind.

"Thou shalt not kill" is, at first glance, a simple moral absolute, but our human ability for rationalisation makes it anything but simple.

Can killing in self-defence, or in a time of war, be compared with murder or abortion?

Yet the act of killing is the same in all cases - life has been taken away from that which had once had life.

And what part does motivation play in this orgy of blood, blurring the lines of demarcation, and complicating still further our reasons for action?

Only an omniscient mind could un-ravel so many different strands of thought and reason and motive, a mind that had brought life into existence in the first place, a mind that had foreseen and understood everything, from the Big Bang and a time of primordial soup, to the plants and animals and humans of the present time.

A strange peace overtook me, and calmness and stillness lay gently on my spirit.

Anger was dissipated, to be replaced by a profound sadness.

I wrote out my sadness, and my pity for the animals, and for the chaos of the world, in poetry.

The Final Court

A looming heap of dark grey stone
With fearsome reputation -
Delivered here was justice true,
To men of every nation,
    The gates stood wide from early morn,
    So all might see the start
    Of this great trial in Heaven's court,
    And all might play their part.
They entered in, by twos and threes,
Until the court was full.
Still more assembled, nervous, hushed,
Until there fell a lull;
    Then silence, like a blanket, lay
    On the assembled crowd.
    Their chatter died, and even whispered
    Talk was not allowed.
They watched in fear as lawyers went
To their allotted places.
Then Peter stood, and saw the suffering

Etched on up-turned faces.
  The Lord High Justice entered last,
  And in the Judgement Seat
  He took his place. The trial began
  With Peter on his feet:
"The man before you stands accused
Of cruelty, and greed.
Will any of you offer help
In this, his hour of need?"
  Attentively, the jury sat,
  The evidence to weigh;
  To hear the twelve whom Peter called
  In turn, throughout the day.
A crippled pig was first to speak:
"You see my joints, so swollen?
He chained me in a sow stall bare.
My health, and life, were stolen,
  And all my piglets, not full grown,
  Knew only concrete floors
  And over-crowded, dirty sheds
  With heavy, metal doors.
They died when only four months old,
And bacon they became.
For sausages, he killed me, then.
My fate, and theirs, the same."
  "I won't save him," quacked the duck,
  "As me, he often ate.
  I feel for him no slightest twinge.
  I care not what his fate."
"I won't save him," clucked the hen,
Her feathers all a-flutter,
"In battery sheds, our bitter lives
Were worse than in the gutter!"
  Another witness took the stand -
  A mournful, gentle cow:
  "He stole my calves, then stole my milk.
  I won't save him now."
A little voice could then be heard,

113

Coming from a fish:
"With trawls and hooks he killed us all,
Our death, his only wish."
 "He ate me as his favourite starter,"
 Squeaked a tiny prawn,
 Whose piercing voice was angry, and
 Betrayed contempt and scorn.
"In fancy glasses we were served,
Drowned in mayonnaise.
He didn't care that this was not
How we should end our days.
 But now his time, like mine, is over.
 Help, I will not give.
 This court decides his punishment,
 If he's to die, or live."
Insects flew, and walked, and crawled,
Of every size and kind;
And for them all, one beetle spoke:
"Excuse, I cannot find
 To let this man escape his judgment.
 Liberally, he sprayed
 Insecticides and herbicides,
 And of his garden made
A cess pit, steeped in chemicals,
His single thought, to kill;
Then birds and hedgehogs, in the food chain,
Ate of us, their fill."
 "In fancy dress he'd chase a fox,
 A pastime he called sport!
 For all the suffering he caused,
 He never spared a thought.
And then, with dogs, he'd hunt me down
'Cross field and hill and dale;
My only hope was saboteurs, and them,
He put in jail!
 I wish, on him, the same grim fate
 As that he wished on me.
 A reason I should help him now,

I really cannot see.
So, in his favour, I won't speak.
I think it's only fair
That of the pain he caused to me,
He now should get his share."
    "The fox and I, we feel the same,"
    Spoke quietly the deer,
    "He showed no pity whilst on earth,
    Why expect it here?
He stalked and shot us, on the hills,
Rejoiced to see us fall.
And my decapitated head
Adorned his study wall!"
    Game birds - pheasant, grouse and quail -
    Whose lives were full of danger,
    Spoke of wealthy country sports:
    "Surely, none was stranger
Than city people, with their guns,
Who blasted from the air
So many birds, who caused no harm.
But this man didn't care."
    A bleating noise could then be heard,
    Coming from a sheep:
    "My place was on the mountain heights,
    Where I could run, and leap.
But this man saw a chance for gain,
By profit, he was led.
His breeding turned us into freaks,
'Just stupid sheep!' he said."
    The twelfth and final witness took
    His place, in that grim court:
    "For Christmas dinners we were bred.
    How cheaply we were bought!
He advertised us everywhere
As making tasty meals.
Contract purchase was our fate,
And supermarket deals.
    Turkey roll became the thing

For everyone to buy.
They didn't know our living hell,
They didn't hear us cry,
They never saw us crammed in sheds,
Mechanically killed;
Just knew us as dismembered pieces,
Stacked on shelves, and chilled."
Of all twelve creatures in that court,
Each one had had their say.
They'd told of lives of misery,
Then sadly gone their way.
Peter, now, addressed the court:
"Is there no one here
To lodge a plea? To mitigate?
Forget the pain and fear,
The suffering he caused you all
In his time on earth.
Can no one find a kindly word?
See nothing that's of worth?"
At last, the Lord High Justice rose,
His judgment to deliver:
"Kindness, shown whilst on the earth
Returns here, to the giver.
But this man worshipped bright, new gods
Of money, power and greed.
He satisfied his appetites,
Indulged his every need.
His animals he left in pain,
Ignored the wounded earth.
Deliberately, he would not see
My miracle of birth.
It only needed one of you
On his behalf, to speak;
To understand his greedy nature,
So indulged, so weak.
Merciful compassion, though,
This man has never shown.
I give my judgment, based on fact.

The evidence, alone,
  Condemns him as a thoughtless man,
  Ruled by worldly pleasure.
  Now, for all his cruelty,
  He will repent at leisure.
The flames of hell await this man,
My mercy he won't see.
He goes to torment without end,
For all eternity."
  The Lord High Justice rose to leave,
  His face deep-lined with sorrow,
  Hoping no more men would face
  This judgment, on the morrow.
With shadowed eyes, great pools of pain,
The court, he left behind.
He knew that happiness, and love,
With animals he'd find.

A very dear friend, who has walked through life beside me for over thirty years, suggested that I should share my thoughts in print.

Leading on from this first, hesitant idea, I met Patricia, and it is entirely through her gentle kindness, and her dynamic energy, that I have reached the last page in the book of my life.

Sitting by the window in my wheelchair, I see the flowers bloom and fade, I watch the birds, endlessly busy with their constant search for food, I marvel as the sun rises and sets, as the moon waxes and wanes, and I keep company in the silence with my own thoughts.

The world is hushed, the fever of life is over, my work is done, and my book is closed at last.

EPILOGUE

Even from its first moment, the candle holder was never "a thing of beauty, a joy for ever, its loveliness increasing."

Unseen at the beginning, it was fatally flawed in its firing by a hairline crack, which darkened and widened with the years, to become an ugly scar across its creation, making it weak and of no value.

The candle it held had burned brightly for so short a time, shedding its light on those who refused to see, offering warmth to those who had no need of it, until its flame faltered and guttered in the wind of the unknown.

Trembling at the gates of eternity, I bid you farewell.